Light of the Bhāgavata

BOOKS by
His Divine Grace
A.C. Bhaktivedanta Swami Prabhupāda

Bhagavad-gītā As It Is
Śrīmad-Bhāgavatam, cantos 1-10 (12 vols.)
Śrī Caitanya-caritāmṛta, (9 vols.)
Teachings of Lord Caitanya
The Nectar of Devotion
The Nectar of Instruction
Śrī Īśopaniṣad
Easy Journey to Other Planets
Kṛṣṇa Consciousness: The Topmost Yoga System
Kṛṣṇa, The Supreme Personality of Godhead
Perfect Questions, Perfect Answers
Teachings of Lord Kapila, the Son of Devahūti
Transcendental Teachings of Prahlāda Mahārāja
Teachings of Queen Kuntī
Kṛṣṇa, the Reservoir of Pleasure
The Science of Self-Realization
The Path of Perfection
Search for Liberation
The Journey of Self-Discovery
A Second Chance
The Laws of Nature
Message of Godhead
Civilization and Transcendence
Renunciation Through Wisdom
Life Comes from Life
The Perfection of Yoga
Beyond Birth and Death
On the Way to Kṛṣṇa
Rāja-vidyā: The King of Knowledge
Elevation to Kṛṣṇa Consciousness
Kṛṣṇa Consciousness: The Matchless Gift
Back to Godhead magazine (founder)

A complete catalogue is available upon request.

BBL Distribution Services
P.O. Box 234, Borehamwood
Herts, WD6 1NB, England
Telephone: 0181-905 1244

The Bhaktivedanta Book Trust
3764 Watseka Avenue
Los Angeles, California 90034
USA

The Bhaktivedanta Book Trust
P.O. Box 262
Botany, N.S.W. 2019
Australia

Light of the Bhāgavata

His Divine Grace
A.C. Bhaktivedanta
Swami Prabhupāda
Founder-Ācārya of the International
Society for Krishna Consciousness

THE BHAKTIVEDANTA BOOK TRUST

Readers interested in the subject matter of this book are invited by the International Society for Krishna Consciousness to correspond with its Secretary at either of the following addresses:

International Society for Krishna Consciousness
P.O. Box 324
Borehamwood Herts. WD6 INB
England
Telephone: 10181-905 1244

International Society for Krishna Consciousness
3764 Watseka Avenue
Los Angeles, California 90034
USA

International Society for Krishna Consciousness
P.O. Box 262
Botany, N.S.W. 2019
Australia

e-mail: bbl@com.bbt.se
www: http:/www. algonet.se/~krishna

ISBN: 91-7149-267-4

Preface

We offer our respectful obeisances unto the lotus feet of His Divine Grace A.C. Bhaktivedanta Swami Prabhupāda, Founder-*Ācārya* of the International Society for Krishna Consciousness, who has delivered the light of the *Bhāgavata* to the whole world. We are pleased to present for his pleasure this publication of his sublime work *Light of the Bhāgavata.*

Of all of His Divine Grace's writings, this work is perhaps unique. It was written in Vrndāvana in 1961 in response to an invitation to attend a world conference, the Congress for Cultivating the Human Spirit, held in Japan. As most of the participants of the conference were from the Orient, Śrīla Prabhupāda considered deeply how he could best present the timeless teachings of *Śrīmad-Bhāgavatam* suitable to the Oriental people. The original *Bhāgavatam* was written over five thousand years ago as an extremely large book composed of eighteen thousand verses. Participants of the conference would not have the time to hear it all. He therefore chose one chapter from the original version for presentation.

The chapter he selected was a description of the autumn season in Vṛndāvana, the place of Lord Kṛṣṇa's appearance. Śrīla Prabhupāda knew that the Oriental people were very fond of hearing descriptions of nature and that the time of the autumn season is particularly auspicious to them. Presenting spiritual philosophy by examples from nature would be best for their understanding. For each seasonal phenomenon, a parallel teaching could be given. For example, the dark, cloudy evening of the rainy autumn season when no stars are visible is compared to the present materialistic, godless civilization when the bright stars of the *Bhāgavata's* wisdom (the devotees and scriptures) are temporarily obscured. Altogether Śrīla Prabhupāda composed forty-eight commentaries to go along with the verses of the chapter.

Śrīla Prabhupāda's plan was that the organizers of the conference should find a qualified Oriental artist to illustrate each verse, and he wrote directions from which the artist could design each painting. He hoped that the paintings and their accompanying explanations would make an impressive display for visitors to the conference. If possible, he wished that there might be published a book containing the illustrations and the texts.

Due to unfortunate circumstances, Śrīla Prabhupāda was unable to attend the conference, and the whole project of *Light of the Bhāgavata* was postponed. In fact, at the time of Śrīla Prabhupāda's disappearance, the *Light of the Bhāgavata* still remained unpublished and the illustrations not yet painted.

The task of completing this great project was therefore left in the hands of the Bhaktivedanta Book Trust, the publishing house dedicated to keeping all of Śrīla Prabhupāda's books in print. Particularly, the work was assigned to the Hong Kong branch of the Book Trust, since Śrīla Prabhupāda had meant the book especially for the Oriental people. After much searching it was our good fortune to secure the help of the renowned artist Madame Li Yun Sheng, whose mature creative talent and sensitive brushwork alone could properly complement Prabhupāda's beautiful descriptions of the autumn season. Undoubtedly, this collection presents the culmination of her long, distinguished career as one of the great artists of modern China. Her Gongbi style of painting together with Śrīla Prabhupāda's poetic descriptions which appear alongside make for a unique blending of the world's two oldest cultural traditions — Indian and Chinese. Thus the beautifully effulgent light of the *Bhāgavata* may now shine upon the world.

—The Publishers

1 ***The arrival of clouds, accompanied by thunder and flashes of lightning all over the sky, provides a picture of life-giving hope. Covered by deep bluish clouds, the sky appears artificially dressed. The thunder and lightning within the clouds are signs of hope for a new way of life.***

The serene sky, limitlessly expansive, is compared to the Absolute Truth. The living entities are truths manifested in relation with the modes of material nature. The deep-bluish cloud covers only an insignificant portion of the limitless sky, and this fractional covering is compared to the quality of ignorance, or forgetfulness of the real nature of the living being. A living entity is as pure as the limitless sky. He becomes covered by the cloud of forgetfulness, however, in his tendency for enjoying the material world. Because of this quality, called *tamas* (ignorance), he considers himself different from the Absolute Whole and forgets his purity, which is like that of the clear sky. This forgetfulness gives rise to separatism in false ego. Thus the forgetful living entities, individually and collectively, make sounds like thundering clouds: 'I am this,' 'It is ours,' or 'It is mine.' This mood of false separatism is called the quality of *rajas*, and it gives rise to a creative force for separate lordship over the mode of *tamas*. The flash of lightning is the only beam of hope that can lead one to the path of knowledge, and therefore it is compared to the mode of *sattva*, or goodness.

The limitless sky, or the all-pervading Absolute Truth (Brahman), is nondifferent from the covered portion of the sky, but simultaneously the whole sky is different from the fractional portion that is liable to be covered by the dark cloud. The cloud, accompanied by thunder and lightning, cannot possibly cover the limitless sky. Therefore the Absolute Truth, which is compared to the whole sky, is simultaneously one with the manifested living being and different from him. The living being is only a sample of the Absolute Truth and is prone to be covered by the circumstantial cloud of ignorance.

There are two parties of philosophers, generally known as the monists and the dualists. The monist believes in the oneness of the Absolute Truth and the living entity, but the dualist believes in the separate identities of the living being and the Absolute Truth. Above these two classes of philosophers is the philosophy of *acintya-bhedābheda tattva,* or the truth of simultaneous oneness and difference. This philosophy was propounded by Lord Śrī Caitanya Mahāprabhu in His explanation of the *Vedānta-sūtras.* The *Vedānta* is the medium of philosophical interpretations, and thus the *Vedānta* cannot be the absolute property of any particular class of philosopher. A sincere seeker of the Absolute Truth is called a Vedāntist. *Veda* means 'knowledge'. Any department of knowledge is called a part of the Vedic knowledge, and *vedānta* means the ultimate conclusion of all branches of knowledge. As philosophy is called the science of all sciences, *Vedānta* is the ultimate philosophy of all philosophical speculations.

***2** The scorching heat of the sun evaporates water from the seas, rivers, lakes, and reservoirs, and there is little water anywhere. The people become thirsty and always look overhead for rain, but in despair. Yet just at the right moment, torrents of rain begin to fall everywhere in the land, even on the hard stones, and the land becomes overflooded.*

The welfare state imposes upon its citizens scorching taxes in various forms — income tax, sales tax, land tax, terminal tax, excise tax, customs tax, and so many other taxes. But in due course, when the taxes accumulate into a large sum of money, they are utilized for the welfare of the citizens in various ways. Nonetheless, sometimes it happens that the benefits of the taxes fall like rains on stone-hearted men in the state who are unable to utilize the money properly and who squander it for sense gratification.

The common man supposes the unequal distribution of rain to represent nature's wrath for our sinful acts. There is truth in this. Thus to have an equal distribution of state-raised taxes, the citizens need to be scrupulously honest and virtuous. They should be honest in the payment of taxes to the state and should have honest representatives to look over the administration. In the modern setup of democratic states the citizens can have no cause for grievances, because the whole administration is conducted by the people themselves. If the people themselves are dishonest, the administrative machinery must be corrupt. Although a damned government of the people may be given a good or fancy name, if the people are not good they cannot have good government, regardless of which party governs the administration. Therefore good character in the consciousness of the mass of people is the first principle necessary for a good government and equal distribution of wealth.

In ancient days the kings were taught lessons in political philosophy by ideal teachers, and the citizens from village to village were taught the principles of self-realization according to the Vedic codes for both the material and the spiritual upliftment of society. Therefore the citizens were God conscious and honest in their dealings, and the kings were responsible for the welfare of the state. The same basic principles are accepted in the democratic governments of the present day, for the irresponsible party of the people is always voted out of power and must yield to the responsible party for a better government. In the cosmic administration there is only one party, which consists of the servants of God, and the responsible deities of the various planets maintain the cosmic laws in terms of the orders of the Supreme Lord. But the people suffer on account of their own folly.

And what is that folly? In *Bhagavad-gītā* it is said that people should perform *yajñas,* or sacrifices for the satisfaction of the Supreme.

annād bhavanti bhūtāni
parjanyād anna-sambhavaḥ
yajñād bhavati parjanyo
yajñaḥ karma-samudbhavaḥ

'All living bodies subsist on food grains, which are produced from rains. Rains are produced by performance of *yajña* [sacrifice], and *yajña* is born of prescribed duties.' (Bg. 3.14)

The Supreme is all-pervading. Therefore people must learn to perform *yajñas* to satisfy the all-pervading Supreme Truth. There are different *yajñas* prescribed for different ages, and in the present age of iron industry the *yajña* that enlightens the mind of the masses for God consciousness is recommended. This process of *yajña* is called the *saṅkīrtana-yajña,* or mass agitation for invoking man's lost spiritual consciousness. As soon as this movement is taken up through spiritual singing, dancing, and feasting, the people will automatically become obedient and honest.

Obedience is the first law of discipline. The people have become disobedient to the laws of God, and therefore neither rain nor wealth is equally distributed. A man who is ultimately disobedient cannot have any good qualifications. When disobedient leaders lead the disobedient people, the whole atmosphere of the administration becomes polluted and full of dangers, as when a blind man leads several other blind men. The state taxes, therefore, should be spent to build the character of the people in general. That will bring happiness to the citizens of the state.

3 ***Attracted by electricity throughout the sky and driven by forceful winds, clouds gradually cover the surface of the earth to satisfy the needy people by supplying water, which is the substance of their life. The clouds bestow rains upon man as the mercy of the Lord, who is always kind to the needy living being.***

We should always know that God is ever kind to us. Despite our gross disobedience to the laws of God's nature, the Lord is kind enough to look after our maintenance. Water is one of the most important items for our maintenance, because without water we can neither produce food grains nor quench our thirst. Water is also required very liberally for many other purposes. Thus the Lord has preserved water on three fourths of the globe and has made it salty to preserve it. Salty water does not decompose, and that is the arrangement of Providence. The Lord has engaged the powerful sun to evaporate the water of planets like earth and distill it into clear water in the clouds and then stock it on the peaks of mountains, as we stock water in overhead tanks for later distribution. Part of the stock of water is refrigerated into ice, so that it will not flood the earth for no good purpose. The ice melts gradually throughout the year, flows down through the great rivers, and glides down to the sea again for preservation.

Therefore the laws of God's nature are neither blind nor accidental, as men with a poor fund of knowledge conclude. Behind the laws of nature is the living brain of God, just as there is always a lawmaker behind all the laws of the state. It does not matter whether or not we see the lawmaker behind the common laws; we must admit that there is a lawmaker. Matter can never work automatically, without a living hand, and therefore we must admit the existence of God, the supreme living being, behind the laws of nature. The Lord says in *Bhagavad-gītā* that nature works under His superintendence.

mayādhyakṣeṇa prakṛtiḥ
sūyate sa-carācaram
hetunānena kaunteya
jagad viparivartate

'This material nature, which is one of My energies, is working under My direction, O son of Kuntī, producing all moving and nonmoving beings. Under its rule this manifestation is created and annihilated again and again.' (Bg. 9.10)

Nature is only a power, and behind the power is a powerhouse and a brain, just as behind electrical power there is an electrical powerhouse, where everything is conducted by the brain of the resident engineer. The material nature works so nicely, and not blindly, because of the superintendence of the supreme powerful God. In the Vedic hymns (*Atharva Veda*) the same thing is confirmed. It is only under the superintendence of God that all the natural laws are conducted.

The Lord distributes His mercy in the form of rains on the scorched earth at times of dire necessity. He supplies rain when we are practically on the verge of death for want of water. God is merciful undoubtedly, but He bestows His mercy on us when we need it most. This is so because we forget God as soon as we obtain this mercy. We should therefore remember the mercy of God constantly if we want to avoid distress. We are eternally related with Him, despite the state of forgetfulness already described above. *Bhagavad-gītā* confirms that the laws of nature are stringent because they are conducted by three different modes. But one who surrenders unto the Lord overcomes the stringency of nature easily. In the *Bhagavad-gītā,* the Lord affirms this:

daivī hy eṣā guṇa-mayī
mama māyā duratyayā
mām eva ye prapadyante
māyām etāṁ taranti te

'This divine energy of Mine, consisting of the three modes of material nature, is difficult to overcome. But those who have surrendered unto Me can easily cross beyond it.' (Bg. 7.14)

4 ***After heavy rain showers, the fields and forests in all directions appear green and healthy. Thus they resemble a man who has undergone severe austerities for some material gain and has achieved his end, for such a man is strong, hearty, and good-looking.***

The greenery of the rainy season is but a temporary show. It looks very pleasant, but we must remember that it will not last. Similarly, there are persons who undergo severe austerities for some material gain, but those who are sane avoid this. Severe austerities for temporary gains are simply a waste of time and energy. Material loss and gain are destined in accordance with the formation of each particular body. There are 8,400,000 species of life, and each type of body is destined to enjoy and suffer in accordance with its particular formation. The bodily enjoyments and sufferings of a wealthy man's son are different from those of a poor man's son. Although no one undergoes severe austerities to obtain distress, it comes upon us uncalled. Similarly, the happiness we are destined to enjoy will come upon us even without our desires.

Even though we may be able to avoid distress and artificially enjoy some material happiness by temporary achievements, this represents no factual gain in life. Our duty is to achieve permanent happiness and eternal life, and it is for that purpose only — for the ultimate gain — that we should undertake all sorts of penances and austerities.

This ultimate gain is possible to achieve in the human form of life. Permanent happiness is possible when one is free from material sources of happiness, for continuation of material bondage means continuation of the threefold miseries. Human life is meant for ending these miseries.

We should not try to be beautiful like seasonal flowers or greenery that flourish in the rainy season but are weary in the winter. To be enlivened by the clouds of ignorance overhead and to enjoy the sight of temporary greenery is not at all desirable. One should try to live in the unlimited clear sky overflooded with the rays of the sun and moon. That is what we actually desire. A life of freedom in eternity, complete knowledge, and a blissful atmosphere is the heart's desire of an enlightened soul. We should undertake all sorts of penances and austerities to attain that permanent source of happiness.

***5** The evening in the rainy season is dark all around. There is no sight of the twinkling stars on the horizon or the pleasing moon. They are covered by clouds. And the insignificant glow-worms become prominent in the absence of the luminaries in the open sky.*

As there are seasonal changes within a year, so there are changing ages in the duration of the manifest cosmic world. These changing ages are called *yugas,* or periods. As there are three modes of nature, there are also various ages dominated by these three modes. The period dominated by the mode of goodness is called Satya-yuga, the period of passion is called Tretā-yuga, the period of mixed passion and ignorance is called Dvāpara-yuga, and the period of darkness and ignorance (the last period) is called Kali-yuga, or the age of quarrel. The word *kali* means 'quarrel'. Kali-yuga is compared to the rainy season because many difficulties in life are experienced during this damp season.

In Kali-yuga there is a dearth of proper guidance. One may take guidance in the evening from the stars and moon, but in the rainy season the light of guidance comes from insignificant glow-worms. The real light in life is the Vedic knowledge. *Bhagavad-gītā* affirms that the purpose of the *Veda* is to know the all-powerful Personality of Godhead.

sarvasya cāhaṁ hṛdi sanniviṣṭo
mattaḥ smṛtir jñānam apohanaṁ ca
vedaiś ca sarvair aham eva vedyo
vedānta-kṛd veda-vid eva cāham

'I am seated in everyone's heart, and from Me come remembrance, knowledge, and forgetfulness. By all the *Vedas,* I am to be known. Indeed, I am the compiler of *Vedānta,* and I am the knower of the *Vedas.*' (Bg. 15.15)

But in this age of quarrel there are quarrels even over the point of the existence of Godhead. In the godless civilization of the age of quarrel there are countless religious societies, religious communities, and religious sects, most of them trying to banish God from religion. Glowworms want to be prominent in the absence of the sun and the stars, and these small groups following various religious conceptions are like glowworms trying to be prominent before the eyes of the ignorant mass of people. There are now a number of self-made incarnations people follow without authority from the Vedic literatures, and there is regular competition between one incarnation's group and another's.

The Vedic knowledge comes in a tradition from the spiritual master through the chain of disciplic succession, and the knowledge must be acquired through this chain, without deviation. In the present age of quarrel the chain has been broken here and there, and thus the *Veda* is now interpreted by unauthorized men who have no realization. The so-called followers of the *Vedas* deny the existence of God, as in the darkness of a cloudy evening the glowworms deny the existence of the moon and stars. Saner people should not be waylaid by such unscrupulous men. *Bhagavad-gītā* is the summary of all Vedic knowledge because it is spoken by the same Personality of Godhead who imparted the Vedic knowledge into the heart of Brahmā, the first created being in the universe. *Śrīmad-Bhāgavatam* was especially spoken for the guidance of the people of this age, which is darkened by the cloud of ignorance.

6 ***On hearing the sound of the torrential rains, the frogs come out of the mountain caves and begin to chant, like brahmacārīs who chant the Vedic hymns by the order of the spiritual master.***

In this age of a godless civilization, the sages of world-recognized religious sects who believe in God must come out of their secluded places and preach the science of God, the Supreme Will, to the people in general. Hindus, Muslims, Christians, and the members of the other sects that have convincing faith in the authority of God must not sit idly now and silently watch the rapid growth of a godless civilization. There is the supreme will of God, and no nation or society can live in peace and prosperity without acceptance of this vital truth.

The warning is already there, and responsible leaders of religious sects must meet together and form a common platform of a league of devotees of the Lord. There is no need for self-realized souls to live in a secluded place. Perfect self-realized souls, engaged in the service of the Lord, are unafraid of *māyā,* just as law-abiding citizens of a state never fear the police. Such fearless devotees of God always speak scientifically about the existence of God, even at the risk of death. Such devotees of God feel compassion for the mass of people, who have completely forgotten the Supreme Lord and who engage in the false pursuit of happiness that ends in the sense pleasures enjoyed by the hogs and dogs.

***7** The small rivulets that almost dried up during the months of May and June now begin to overflow their banks, like upstarts that suddenly overflow the limits of expenditure.*

One should learn gravity from the sea and the rivulet. The sea is always within its limits, in spite of the many rivers pouring water into it. Similarly, one should properly use the assets of life and not squander them for purposes that have no permanent value. Uncontrolled, sensuous persons play with the assets of the body and accumulate wealth. But the strength of the body should be used for self-realization, not for sense gratification.

Human beings have two kinds of temperament. Some are introspective, and the others are extravagant. Those who are extravagant are enamoured of the external features of phenomenal beauty and have no insight into the whole manifestation. They are practically asleep to introspection, and thus they are unable to derive any permanent value from the assets of the human form of body. But one who has developed introspection is as grave as the sea. While those who are extravagant are calm and quiet in sleep, such grave persons use the full advantage of the human form of life.

Although the animal propensities of the body should be minimized, those who are extravagant temporarily overflow in material enjoyment. Nonetheless, as soon as the rainy season of life is over, they become as dry as dry river beds. Life is meant for the right cause, or *sat* — that which exists for all time. In the material world, nothing is *sat*, or eternal, but the bad bargain of the material world can be used for the best purpose. The mind dedicated to extravagance is a bad bargain, but one can make the best use of the mind by introspection.

8 ***The colourful greenery of the newly grown grass, the seasonal flowers, the frog's umbrellas, the butterflies, and the other variegatedness of the rainy season perfectly represent a well-to-do family absorbed in vanity over their personal assets.***

A rich man displays his opulence in various colourful ways. He has a good residential bungalow with sufficient property and a well-trimmed garden. The bungalow is decorated with up-to-date furniture and carpets. There are motorcars with dazzling polish, and a radio set receiving and broadcasting colourful news and melodious songs. All these captivate their proprietor as though he were in a dreamland of his own creation.

When the same man was as dry as fallow land and had none of these opulences, he was plain in behaviour, but since obtaining all these material means of enjoyment he has forgotten the principle that everything in the world comes and goes away like the changing seasons. The beautiful Red Fort and the Taj Mahal were built by Shah Jahan, who left the place long ago, and many others have also come and gone in the same place, like seasonal flowers. Material assets are like seasonal flowers only. Either the flowers wither, or the gardener himself leaves. This is the law of nature. Therefore, if we want permanent life, knowledge, and bliss, we must seek them somewhere else, not in the changeable, temporary rainy season, which is flooded with so many varieties of pleasing sights that vanish when the season ends.

Material manifestations of things are but shadowy representations of reality. They are compared to mirages in the desert. In the desert there is no water, but the foolish deer runs after illusory water in the desert to quench its thirsty heart. Water is not unreal, but the place where we seek it is misleading. The advancement of materialistic civilization is just like a mirage in the desert. The deer runs after water in the desert with full speed, and the illusion of water moves ahead at the same speed as the foolish deer. Water is not false, but we must not seek it in the desert. A living entity, by his past experience, remembers the real happiness of his original, spiritual existence, but since he has forgotten himself he seeks spiritual or permanent happiness in matter, although this is impossible to achieve.

9 ***A picturesque scene of green paddy fields enlivens the heart of the poor agriculturalist, but it brings gloom to the face of the capitalist who lives by exploiting the poor farmers.***

With good rains, the farmer's business in agriculture flourishes. Agriculture is the noblest profession. It makes society happy, wealthy, healthy, honest, and spiritually advanced for a better life after death. The *vaiśya* community, or the mercantile class of men, take to this profession. In *Bhagavad-gītā* the *vaiśyas* are described as the natural agriculturalists, the protectors of cows, and the general traders. When Lord Śrī Kṛṣṇa incarnated Himself at Vṛndāvana, He took pleasure in becoming a beloved son of such a *vaiśya* family. Nanda Mahārāja was a big protector of cows, and Lord Śrī Kṛṣṇa, as the most beloved son of Nanda Mahārāja, used to tend His father's animals in the neighbouring forest. By His personal example Lord Kṛṣṇa wanted to teach us the value of protecting cows. Nanda Mahārāja is said to have possessed nine hundred thousand cows, and at the time of Lord Śrī Kṛṣṇa (about five thousand years ago) the tract of land known as Vṛndāvana was flooded with milk and butter. Therefore God's gifted professions for mankind are agriculture and cow protection.

Trade is meant only for transporting surplus produce to places where the produce is scanty. But when traders become too greedy and materialistic they take to large-scale commerce and industry and allure the poor agriculturalist to unsanitary industrial towns with a false hope of earning more money. The industrialist and the capitalist do not want the farmer to remain at home, satisfied with his agricultural produce. When the farmers are satisfied by a luxuriant growth of food grains, the capitalist becomes gloomy at heart. But the real fact is that humanity must depend on agriculture and subsist on agricultural produce. No one can produce rice and wheat in big iron factories. The industrialist goes to the villagers to purchase the food grains he is unable to produce in his factory. The poor agriculturalist takes advances from the capitalist and sells his produce at a lower price. Hence when food grains are produced abundantly the farmers become financially stronger, and thus the capitalist becomes morose at being unable to exploit them.

10 ***Just as a living being attains a transcendentally attractive form by rendering service to Lord Hari, similarly, all the inhabitants of the land and the water assume beautiful forms by taking advantage of the newly fallen water.***

We have practical experience of this with our students in the International Society for Krishna Consciousness. Before becoming students, they were dirty-looking, although they had naturally beautiful personal features; but due to having no information of Kṛṣṇa consciousness they appeared very dirty and wretched. Since they have taken to Kṛṣṇa consciousness, their health has improved, and by following the rules and regulations, their bodily lustre has increased. When they are dressed with saffron-coloured cloth, with *tilaka* on their foreheads and beads in their hands and on their necks, they look exactly as if they come directly from Vaikuṇṭha.

The residents of the water are the fish, frogs, and so on, and the residents of the land are the cows, deer, and so on. By constantly drinking and taking bath in the fresh rainwater of the rainy season, the tired and parched animals are refreshed, and their complexions become brilliant as their health is invigorated by the arrival of new rainwater. The lakes, ponds, and rivers are cleansed and invigorated by the downpour of new rainwater and thus become most beautiful. Similarly, a devotee of the Supreme Lord who takes advantage of the beautiful and invigorating downpour of the transcendental descriptions of God found in Vedic literature finds his spiritual consciousness invigorated and refreshed. In this way his spiritualized body becomes very beautiful.

***11** In the rainy season, when the rivers swell and rush to the ocean, and as the wind blows the waves about, the ocean appears to be agitated. Similarly, if a person engaged in the mystic yoga process is not very advanced in spiritual life, he can be affected by the modes of nature and thus will be agitated by the sex impulse.*

A person fixed in spiritual knowledge will not be attracted by the allurement of material nature in the form of beautiful women and the sex pleasure enjoyed in their association. One, however, who is still immature in the cultivation of spiritual knowledge may be attracted at any moment by the illusion of temporary happiness, just as the ocean is agitated by the rushing rivers and blowing wind that occur during the rainy season. It is therefore very important to fix oneself at the lotus feet of a bona fide spiritual master who is a representative of God so that one will not be carried away by sex agitation.

12 The mountains, although being struck by torrents of rain during the rainy season, are not shaken, just as those whose hearts are dedicated to the transcendental Personality of Godhead are never disturbed, even when harassed by great misfortune.

Because a person who is spiritually advanced accepts any adverse condition of life as the mercy of the Lord, he is completely eligible to enter into the spiritual kingdom. Even though a person takes to the devotional service of the Supreme Lord, he may sometimes become diseased, impoverished, or disappointed by life's events. A true devotee of the Lord always considers these sufferings to be due to past sinful activities, and thus without becoming disturbed he patiently awaits the mercy of the Supreme Lord. Such devotees are compared to high mountains, which are never agitated in any way, even when struck by powerful torrents of rain in the rainy season. Rather, such devotees remain humble in spiritual enlightenment. Free from pride and envy, they easily gain the mercy of the Lord and go back home, back to Godhead.

***13** In the rainy season some of the roads are not frequently used and become covered with long grasses, and thus it becomes very difficult to see the road. Similarly, in this age the transcendental scriptures are not properly studied by the brāhmaṇas. Being covered by the effects of time, the scriptures are practically lost, and it becomes very difficult to understand or follow them.*

A covered road is exactly like a *brāhmaṇa* who is not accustomed to studying and practising the reformatory practices of Vedic injunctions — he becomes covered with the long grasses of illusion. In that condition, forgetful of his constitutional nature, he forgets his position of eternal servitorship to the Supreme Personality of Godhead. By being deviated by the seasonal overgrowth of long grasses created by *māyā,* a person identifies himself with illusory productions of nature and succumbs to illusion, forgetting his spiritual life.

***14** The lightning becomes unsteady in its friendship, failing to remain faithfully in any one of the clouds, although they are the friends of the entire world, just as lusty women do not remain steady even in the company of men who possess excellent qualities.*

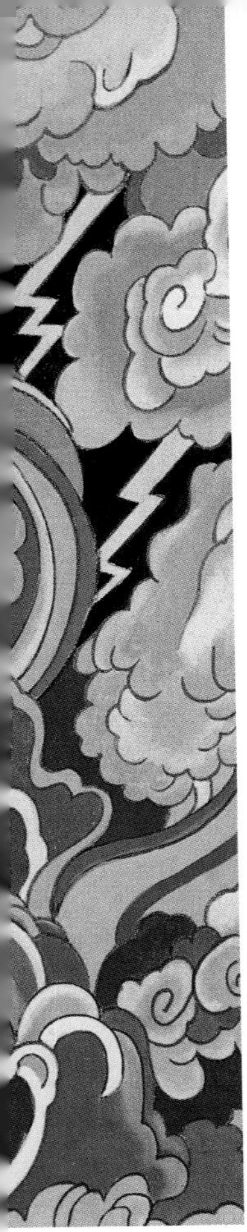

During the rainy season, lightning appears in one group of clouds and then immediately in another group of clouds. This phenomenon is compared to a lusty woman who does not fix her mind on one man. A cloud is compared to a qualified person because it pours rain and gives sustenance to many people; a man who is qualified similarly gives sustenance to many living creatures, such as family members or many workers in business. Unfortunately, his whole life can be disturbed by a wife who divorces him. When the husband is disturbed, the whole family is ruined, the children are dispersed, or the business is closed, and everything is affected. It is therefore recommended that a woman desiring to advance in Kṛṣṇa consciousness peacefully live with a husband and that the couple should not separate under any condition. The husband and wife should control sex indulgence and concentrate their minds on Kṛṣṇa consciousness so their lives may be successful. After all, in the material world a man requires a woman, and a woman requires a man. When they are combined, they should live peacefully in Kṛṣṇa consciousness and should not be restless, like the lightning flashing from one group of clouds to another.

***15** In the midst of the thunder in the cloudy sky there appears a rainbow that has no string. Its appearance is compared to the appearance of the Supreme Personality of Godhead or His servants in the midst of the material atmosphere.*

The Sanskrit word *guṇa* means 'quality' or 'mode', as well as string or rope. When a rainbow appears during the rainy season, it is observed to be like a bow with no *guṇa*, or string. Similarly, the appearance of the Personality of Godhead or His transcendental servants has nothing to do with the qualitative modes of material nature. The phenomenal appearance of the Transcendence is free from the qualities of material nature, and thus it resembles a bow with no string.

The transcendental Supreme Lord is eternally the form of transcendental existence, knowledge, and bliss. The material energy works under His good will, and therefore He is never affected by the modes of material nature. When He appears before us in the midst of material interactions, He remains always unaffected, like a stringless rainbow.

By His inconceivable energy, the Supreme Lord can appear and disappear like a rainbow, which appears and disappears without being affected by the roaring thunder and the cloudy sky. The Lord is eternally the biggest of the big and the smallest of the small. The living beings, who are His parts and parcels, are the smallest of the small, and He is the biggest of the big as the Absolute Truth, the Supreme Personality of Godhead.

16 ***At night, by the grace of the moonlight, the clouds in the sky can be seen moving. Yet the moon itself also appears to be moving, just as a living being appears to be moving because of false identification with matter.***

At night in the rainy season the moving clouds reflecting the moonlight make the moon appear to be moving. This is called illusion. The spirit soul, or the living being, is the root of all the activities of the material body, but because of illusion the spirit soul remains covered by the gross and subtle material bodies. Thus covered, the conditioned soul identifies with the material body and becomes subject to the sense of false ego.

This false ego obliges a living being to consider his material body to be his self, the offspring of the body to be his children, and the land of the birth of the body to be an object of worship. Thus the living being's conception of nationalism is another type of ignorance. Because of ignorance, a living being identifies himself with the land of his birth and moves with the misconceptions of national ideas. In fact, however, a living being does not belong to any nation or species of life. He has nothing to do with the body, as the moon has nothing to do with the moving clouds.

The moon is far away from the clouds and is fixed in its own orbit, but illusion presents a scene in which the moon appears to be moving. A living being should not float with the misconception of the temporary body; he must always know himself to be transcendental to the bodily identity. This is the path of knowledge, and complete knowledge fixes the living being in the orbit of spiritual activities.

The spiritual living force is always active by nature. By illusion his activities are wrongly directed in relation with the body, but in the liberated condition of complete knowledge his activities are conducted in spiritual devotion. Liberation does not mean stopping activities; it means being purified of illusory activities and becoming transcendental to relations with the gross and subtle bodies.

17 When the clouds appear in the sky, the peacock begins to dance in ecstasy, as a sincere soul becomes overwhelmed with joy on the appearance of a saint at his house.

The duty of sages and saints is to go from door to door and thus enlighten the householders in spiritual knowledge. Householder life is compared to a dark well. In a dark well the frog cannot see the free light of the open sky. The dark well of householder life kills the soul. One should therefore get out of it so that he may see the light of spiritual vision. Saints and sages mercifully try to uplift fallen souls from the dark well of householder life. An enlightened householder therefore takes pleasure in the appearance of such saints and sages at his house. The mind of the householder who is a conditioned soul is always disturbed by the threefold miseries of material life. Everyone wants to be happy in his householder life, but the laws of nature do not allow one to become happy in material existence, which is like a spontaneous forest fire.

In the age of Kali, as described before, people in general no longer take pleasure in the presence of saints and sages, nor are they interested in spiritual enlightenment. The saints and sages, however, take all risks to propagate the message of Godhead. Lord Jesus Christ, Ṭhākura Haridāsa, Lord Nityānanda Prabhu, and many such sages risked their life to propagate the message of Godhead. Self-realized saints and sages take such risks for the spiritual enlightenment of the people in general. They do not take vows of silence meant to win cheap glory from the ignorant mass of people. God is satisfied only when His devotees take all sorts of risks to propagate His glories. Such devotees are unafraid of the difficult journey to cross the ocean of nescience. They are always anxious for the welfare of the fallen souls, who are attached to the false enjoyment of materialistic life, in which they forget their eternal relation with God.

It is the duty of the saints and sages to enlighten the fallen souls, and reciprocally it is the duty of the householder to receive the saints and sages cordially, as the peacock dances in ecstasy at the presence of clouds in the sky. The fire of threefold miseries experienced by materialistic men can be extinguished only by the cloud of mercy of the saints and sages who can pour down the water of transcendental messages to put an end to the miseries of the householders.

18 Many plants and creepers that were almost dead during the months of April and May are now visible again in various forms, for they are nourished by their roots in the moist earth. These numberless plants and creepers resemble persons who dry up in severe penances for some material gain but then achieve their objectives and become luxuriously fat, nourished by sense enjoyment.

In *Bhagavad-gītā* it is said that when the daytime of Brahmā is over, the manifested creations of the universe all vanish, and after the end of Brahmā's night the creation is manifested again.

Thus the cosmic creation, in its manifestation and nonmanifestation, resembles the creepers and plants that appear during the rainy season and gradually vanish when the season is over.

bhūta-grāmaḥ sa evāyaṁ
bhūtvā bhūtvā pralīyate
rātry-āgame 'vaśaḥ pārtha
prabhavaty ahar-āgame

'Again and again, when Brahmā's day arrives, all living entities come into being, and with the arrival of Brahma's night they are helplessly annihilated.' (Bg. 8.19)

Even when the plants and creepers are no longer to be seen, their seeds remain, and these dormant seeds fructify in contact with water. Similarly, the seedlike spiritual sparks who are dominated by the desire to lord it over the material nature exist in a dormant state after the cosmic manifestation is annihilated; and when the cosmic manifestation reappears, all the silent living beings within the womb of material nature come out and engage in sense enjoyment, thereby growing luxuriously fat.

To attain liberation, one must be completely purified of perverted forms of desire. A living being cannot snuff out desires, and to practise artificially erasing the actions of desire is more dangerous than the active desires themselves. All desires should be reformed and directed toward spiritual activities; otherwise those same desires will repeatedly manifest themselves in different varieties of material enjoyment, thus conditioning the living being perpetually in material bondage.

19 *A crane stands on the edge of a pond that is always disturbed by flowing water, mud, and stones. The crane is like a householder who is disturbed in the shelter of his home but who, because of too much attachment, does not want to change his position.*

The forgetful householder life of the conditioned soul is a soul-killing dark well. This is the opinion of Śrī Prahlāda Mahārāja, the celebrated devotee of the Lord. Too much attachment for hearth and home is never recommended by a self-realized soul. Therefore the span of human life should be methodically divided.

The first stage is called the *brahmacarya-āśrama,* or the order of life in childhood, when the man-to-be is trained in the ultimate goal of life. The next stage is the *gṛhastha-āśrama,* in which the man is trained to enter into the Transcendence. Then comes the *vānaprastha-āśrama,* the preliminary stage of renounced life. The last stage recommended is the *sannyāsa* order, or the renounced order of life. In this way one accepts a gradual process of spiritual activities for the ultimate goal of liberation.

Unfortunately, for want of sufficient culture of the human spirit, no one wants to give up the householder life, even though it is full of pinpricks and mud. And those who are too attached amidst the pinpricks of muddy householder life are compared to the cranes that stand on the bank of the river for some sense enjoyment despite all the inconveniences there. We should always remember that the society, friendship, and love we are supposed to enjoy in family life are only shadowy representations of the real society, friendship, and love reciprocated in the kingdom of God. There is no reality in the conditioned life of material existence, but because of our ignorance we are attached to the mirage. The idea of society, friendship, and love is not at all false, but the place where we search for it is false. We have to give up this false position and rise to the reality. That should be the aim of life, and that is the result of cultivating the human spirit.

Unfortunately, for want of sufficient culture of this spirit, the materialistic man always sticks to this false place in spite of all its turmoils. It is said that a man should give up the order of householder life at the age of fifty. But in this era of ignorance even an old man wants to rejuvenate his bodily functions, put on artificial teeth, and make a pretense of youthful life, even on the verge of death. Cranelike politicians especially are too much attached to the false prestige of position and rank, and so they always seek reelection, even at the fag end of life. These are some of the symptoms of an uncultured life.

20 ***Fierce torrents of rain break over the strands and the partition walls of the paddy field. These disturbances resemble those created by the seasonal opponents of the standard principles of the Vedas, who are influenced by the age of Kali.***

Originally the path of self-realization was established by the standard direction of the *Vedas.* Śrīla Vyāsadeva divided the original *Veda* into four divisions, namely *Sāma, Atharva, Ṛg,* and *Yajur.* Then he divided the same *Vedas* into eighteen *Purāṇas* (supplements) and the *Mahābhārata,* and then again the same author summarized them in the *Vedānta-sūtras.* The purpose of all these Vedic literatures is to realize one's self to be a spiritual being, eternally related with the Supreme Personality of Godhead, the all-attractive form (Śrī Kṛṣṇa).

But all these different Vedic literatures were systematically distorted by the onslaught of the age of Kali, as the walls of the paddy field and the strand of the river are distorted by the onslaught of heavy rains. The attacks of distortion are offered by atheistic philosophers who are concerned only with eating, drinking, being merry, and enjoying. These atheists are all against the revealed scriptures because such persons are intimately attached to sense pleasures and gross materialism. There are also others who do not believe in the eternity of life. Some of them propose that life is ultimately to be annihilated and that only the material energy is conserved. Others are less concerned with physical laws but do not believe anything beyond their experience. And still others equate spirit and matter and declare the distinction between them to be illusory.

There is no doubt that the *Vedas* stand as the most recognized books of knowledge, from every angle of vision. But over the course of time the Vedic path has been attacked by philosophers like Cārvāka, Buddha, Arhat, Kapila, Patañjali, Śaṅkara, Vaikāraṇa, Jaimini, the Nyāyakas, the Vaiśeṣikas, the Saguṇists, the empiricists, the Pāśupata Śaivas, the Saguṇa Śaivas, the Brāhmas, the Āryas, and many others (the list of non-Vedic speculators grows daily, without restriction). The path of the *Vedas* does not accord with any principle devoid of an eternal relation with God, attainment of His devotional service, and culmination in transcendental love for Him.

21 ***The wind carries the clouds to different parts of the globe, and the clouds distribute rains, to the satisfaction of the people in general, just as rich kings and merchants distribute their accumulated wealth, inspired by religious priests.***

As already explained, the four divisions of society — namely the intelligent class of men (the *brāhmaṇas*), the ruling class (the *kṣatriyas*), the mercantile class (the *vaiśyas*), and the labouring class (the *śūdras*) — are meant to achieve one goal in life: self-realization, or cultivation of the human spirit. The intelligent class of men, the *brāhmaṇas,* are to inspire the *kṣatriyas* and *vaiśyas* in performing sacrifices for spiritual cultivation, and thus the cooperation of the *brāhmaṇas, kṣatriyas,* and *vaiśyas* uplifts the people in general, or the ordinary labouring class of men. As soon as this cooperation between the four classes of men in society stops and the basic principles of spiritual culture are neglected, the social structure of humanity becomes a second edition of animal life, based on the propensities of eating, sleeping, fearing, and mating. It is the duty of the intelligent men to influence the members of the richer communities — the *kṣatriyas* and *vaiśyas* — to sacrifice for spiritual culture. Only in this way can the tension between the capitalists and the labourers be well mitigated.

In this age of Kali, when a slight difference of opinion leads to quarrel, even to the extent of riots, it is the duty of the intelligent men, the *brāhmaṇas,* to selflessly inspire the richer people to sacrifice for this purpose. It is suggested herewith that the men of the intelligent class should not themselves try to become *kṣatriyas* or *vaiśyas,* nor should they engage themselves in the occupations of the various other classes; rather, the *brāhmaṇas* should simply guide them in spiritual cultivation, just as the wind carries the clouds to other places to pour water. The wind itself does not take up the responsibility for pouring water.

The most intelligent men in society are the saints and sages who have sacrificed everything for the service of spiritual culture. Their duty is to travel throughout human society and inspire its members to engage themselves in acts of spiritual culture by sacrificing their words, money, intelligence, and life. That should be the theme of human life in order to make it a complete success. A society with no taste for spiritual culture is a blazing fire, and everyone in that fire perpetually suffers the threefold miseries. As clouds pour water on a blazing fire in the forest and thus extinguish it, the intelligent men who work as the spiritual masters of society pour water on the blazing fire of miseries by disseminating spiritual knowledge and inspiring the richer section of the society to help in the cause. Temples of worship, for example, are constructed by the rich, and these temples are meant to impart spiritual education to people in general. The periodic spiritual ceremonies are held for inspiration, and not for exploitation. If there are flaws now because of the age of Kali, they should be rectified, but the institutions must be saved.

22 ***After the complete rainy season, the forest of Vṛndāvana was full of fruits like dates and blackberries ripening on the trees and bushes. Lord Śrī Kṛṣṇa, along with His elder brother, Śrī Baladeva, and other cowherd boys of the vicinity, entered the beautiful forest, accompanied by the cows, to display transcendental pastimes with His eternal friends.***

Lord Śrī Kṛṣṇa, the Supreme Personality of Godhead, appears with His personal entourage once in 4,320,000,000 years and displays His transcendental paraphernalia, just to attract the conditioned souls of the material world. Although the material world is only a shadow of the spiritual world, the materially encaged living entities seek spiritual happiness here in a form perverted by materialistic attachment. Empiric philosophers with a poor fund of knowledge imagine a spiritual picture that is impersonal. But the spiritual living being, less attracted by the impersonal form of spiritual emancipation, becomes more attracted by the material form and becomes hopeless of spiritual emancipation.

Therefore the Absolute Personality of Godhead, out of His limitless and causeless mercy, descends from the spiritual kingdom and displays His personal pastimes at Vṛndāvana, the replica of the Kṛṣṇaloka planet in the spiritual sky. Vṛndāvana is the most sacred place within this cosmic universe, and people seeking to achieve spiritual emancipation by entering the kingdom of God may make a home at Vṛndāvana and become serious students of the six Gosvāmīs, who were instructed by Lord Śrī Caitanya Mahāprabhu. The six Gosvāmīs were headed by Śrīla Rūpa Gosvāmī, who was followed by Śrīla Sanātana, Śrīla Bhaṭṭa Raghunātha, Śrīla Jīva, Śrīla Gopāla Bhaṭṭa, and Śrīla Raghunātha dāsa Gosvāmī. They were all seriously engaged in research and excavation of the mystery of Vṛndāvana-dhāma.

Lord Śrī Kṛṣṇa, the Supreme Personality of Godhead, appeared at Vṛndāvana about five thousand years ago, and the relics of His appearance at Vṛndāvana were lost from view. But Lord Śrī Caitanya Mahāprabhu, who is the very same Lord Śrī Kṛṣṇa in the form of a great devotee, appeared at Navadvīpa, a district in West Bengal, and excavated the holy places of Lord Śrī Kṛṣṇa's transcendental pastimes. He instructed the above-mentioned six Gosvāmīs to compose authorized literature on the cult of Vṛndāvana, and any serious student anxious to know about the Supreme Lord may take advantage of this invaluable literature and the guidance of authorized scholars and thus know about the Lord of Vṛndāvana, Śrī Kṛṣṇa, the Personality of Godhead.

After the complete rainy season, the forest of Vṛndāvana was full of fruits like dates and blackberries ripening on the trees and bushes. Lord Śrī Kṛṣṇa, along with His elder brother, Śrī Baladeva, and other cowherd boys of the vicinity, entered the beautiful forest, accompanied by the cows, to display transcendental pastimes with His eternal friends.

***23** The cows that followed the Lord within the forest moved slowly because of their heavy, milk-laden udders. But when the Lord called them by their specific names they at once became alert, and as they hastened toward Him their milk bags overflowed and poured milk on the ground because of affection for the Lord.*

It is understood from scriptures like the *Brahma-saṁhitā* that in the spiritual abode of the Lord the houses are made of touchstone and the trees are all desire trees. There the Lord is accustomed to tending thousands and thousands of *kāmadhenus* (cows able to supply unlimited quantities of milk). And all the houses, trees, and cows are qualitatively nondifferent from the Lord. The Lord and His paraphernalia in the spiritual abode are one and the same in quality, although there are differences for the pleasure of the Lord. In the material world also we have various paraphernalia for our pleasures in life, but because all this paraphernalia is made of matter, it is all destructible at the end. In the spiritual sky there are the very same varieties of pleasure, but they are all meant for the Lord. There the Lord alone is the supreme enjoyer and beneficiary, and all others are enjoyed by the Lord. The Lord is served there by all kinds of servitors, and both the master and the servitors are of the same quality. This spiritual variegatedness is displayed by the Lord when He descends at Vṛndāvana, and we may know that the Lord descends with His personal staff of cows, cowherd boys, and cowherd maidens, all of whom are but spiritual expansions of the Lord Himself for His own pleasures. Thus when called by the Lord the cows were overwhelmed by joyous affection, just as the mother's breast overflows with milk when the child cries for it.

All of us living beings are differentiated expansions of the Lord, but our affection for the Lord is submerged within us, artificially covered by the material quality of ignorance. Spiritual culture is meant to revive this natural affection of the living being for the Lord. The ingredients of fire are already present in safety matches, and only mild friction is needed to ignite a fire. Similarly, our natural affection for the Lord has to be revived by a little culture. Specifically, we have to receive the messages of the Lord with a purified heart.

For spiritual realization one has to purify the heart and know things in their true perspective. As soon as one does this, the flow of one's natural affection begins to glide toward the Lord, and with the progress of this flow one becomes more and more self-realized in various relations with the Lord. The Lord is the centre of all the affection of all living beings, who are all His parts and parcels. When the flow of natural affection for the Lord is clogged by desires to imitate His Lordship, one is said to be in *māyā,* or illusion. *Māyā* has no substantial existence, but as long as its hallucinations go on, their reactions are felt. The Lord, by His causeless mercy, displays the reality of life so that our hallucinations may be completely dissipated.

***24** When the Lord entered the forest of Vṛndāvana, all the inhabitants of the forest, both animate and inanimate, were eager to receive Him. He saw that the flowers of the forest, all fully blossoming, were weeping in ecstasy, honey flowing down their petals. The waterfalls on the hilly rocks were gladly flowing, and one could hear sweet sounds from the caves nearby.*

The Lord has multifarious energies, and therefore the Lord and His energies are identical. Among His various energies the material energy is one, and it is said in the *Bhagavad-gītā* that the material energy is inferior in quality to the spiritual energy. Spiritual energy is superior because without contact with the spiritual energy the material energy alone cannot produce anything. But the source of all energies is the all-attractive Personality of Godhead, Śrī Kṛṣṇa.

This material world is a combination of matter and spirit, but the spiritual world, which is far, far away from the material sky, is purely spiritual and has no contact with matter. In the spiritual world, everything is spirit. We have already discussed this. The Personality of Godhead, the original source of all energies, is able to convert spirit into matter and matter into spirit. For Him there is no difference between matter and spirit. He is therefore called *kaivalya*.

In Lord Śrī Kṛṣṇa's transcendental pastimes, He reciprocates with spirit, not matter. When He is in the mortal world, the material qualities cannot work upon Him. An electrician knows how to take work from electricity. With the help of electricity he can turn water into cold or heat. Similarly, the Personality of Godhead can turn matter into spirit and spirit into matter by His inconceivable power. Everything is therefore matter and spirit by the grace of the Almighty, although there is a difference between matter and spirit for the ordinary living being.

Flowers, waterfalls, trees, fruits, hills, caves, birds, beasts, and human beings are nothing but combinations of God's energy. Therefore when the Personality of Godhead appeared before them they all became spiritually inclined, and by natural affection they wanted to serve the Almighty in various capacities.

There are different stages of spiritual development in matter. In the material world the spiritual sparks of the Personality of Godhead are covered by the material energy in different proportions, and gradually they become spiritualized in various species of life. The human form of life represents the complete development of the senses for spiritual realization of one's original affection for the Lord. Therefore if despite this opportunity for human life we are unable to revive our natural affection for the Lord, we must know that we are wasting our lives for nothing. By the grace of the Lord, however, the spiritual consciousness of every species of life can occupy its proper place, and these species can express their spiritual affection for the Lord in the *śānta-rasa,* as displayed by the land, water, hills, trees, fruits, and flowers of Vṛndāvana during the presence of Lord Śrī Kṛṣṇa, the Personality of Godhead.

25 ***The Lord reciprocated the feelings of the inhabitants of the forest of Vṛndāvana. When there was rainfall, the Lord took shelter at the feet of the trees or in the caves and enjoyed the taste of different fruits with His eternal associates the cowherd boys. He played with them, sat with them, and ate fruits with them.***

Becoming one with God does not always indicate that a living being merges into the existence of the Lord. To become one with God means to attain one's original, spiritual quality. Unless one attains one's spiritual quality one cannot enter into the kingdom of God. The members of the impersonalist school explain their idea of oneness by the example of the mixing of river water with the seawater. But we should know that within the water of the sea there are living beings, who do not merge into the existence of water but keep their separate identities and enjoy life within the water. They are one with the water in the sense that they have attained the quality of living within the water. Similarly, the spiritual world is not without its separate paraphernalia. A living being can keep his separate spiritual identity in the spiritual kingdom and enjoy life with the supreme spiritual being, the Personality of Godhead.

In Vṛndāvana all the spiritual entities — the cowherd boys, the cow maids, the forest, the trees, the hills, the water, the fruits, the cows, and all others — enjoy life spiritually in association with the Lord, Śrī Kṛṣṇa. They are simultaneously one with and different from the Lord. But ultimately they are one in different varieties.

26 ***The Lord enjoyed in the company of Lord Baladeva and the other cowherd boys and sometimes sat with them on the same stone slab. While sitting they ate simple food like rice, dhal, vegetables, bread, and curd, which they had brought from their homes and which they shared in friendly exchanges.***

In *Bhagavad-gītā* the Lord has expressed His willingness to accept fruit, flowers, leaves, and water from His devotee when they have been offered to Him in devotional affection. The Lord can eat anything and everything, because everything is but a transformation of His own energy. But when there is a question of offering Him something, the offerings must be within the range of the eatables the Lord has ordered. We cannot offer the Lord that which He has not ordered. The Personality of Godhead, Śrī Kṛṣṇa, cannot be offered anything beyond the range of good foodstuffs like rice, *dhal,* wheat, vegetables, milk and milk preparations, and sugar. At Jagannātha Purī the Lord is offered such foodstuffs, and in all scriptures the very same foodstuffs are mentioned everywhere.

The Lord is never hungry, nor does He require any food to fill His empty stomach. He is complete in Himself. Yet He always mercifully eats the foods offered by His devotees in sincere affection. The cowherd boys brought simple foodstuffs from home, and the Lord, who is constantly served by hundreds and thousands of goddesses of fortune, is always glad to accept such simple foodstuffs from His devotee friends. All the relatives of the Lord are His devotees only, and they are situated in different transcendental mellows as friends, parents, and lovers. The Lord derives transcendental pleasure by accepting services from His various grades of devotees, who are situated in various grades of *rasas.* These transcendental *rasas* are pervertedly reflected in the material atmosphere, and thus the spiritual living being, out of ignorance only, vainly seeks the same bliss in matter.

27 *After good rains the grazing ground for the animals was full of green pasture, and both the bulls and the cows sat down on the grass fully satisfied. The cows, followed by their calves, appeared tired of grazing, because of full milk bags. Calmly and quietly the cows and calves rested and ruminated, chewing their cud.*

Protection and grazing ground for the cows are among the essential needs for society and the welfare of people in general. The animal fat required for the human body can be well derived from cow's milk. Cow's milk is very important for human energy, and the economic development of society depends on sufficient food grains, sufficient milk, and sufficient transportation and distribution of these products. Lord Śrī Kṛṣṇa, by His personal example, taught us the importance of cow protection, which is meant not only for the Indian climate but for all human beings all over the universe.

Less intelligent people underestimate the value of cow's milk. Cow's milk is also called *gorasa,* or the juice from the body of the cow. Milk is the most valuable form of *gorasa,* and from milk we can prepare many important and valuable foodstuffs for the upkeep of the human body. The killing of cows by human society is one of the grossest suicidal policies, and those who are anxious to cultivate the human spirit must turn their attention first toward the question of cow protection.

If we really want to cultivate the human spirit in society we must have first-class intelligent men to guide the society, and to develop the finer tissues of our brains we must assimilate vitamin values from milk. Devotees worship Lord Śrī Kṛṣṇa by addressing Him as the well-wisher of the *brāhmaṇas* and the cows. The most intelligent class of men, who have perfectly attained knowledge in spiritual values, are called the *brāhmaṇas.* No society can improve in transcendental knowledge without the guidance of such first-class men, and no brain can assimilate the subtle form of knowledge without fine brain tissues. For such important brain tissues we require a sufficient quantity of milk and milk preparations. Ultimately, we need to protect the cow to derive the highest benefit from this important animal. The protection of cows, therefore, is not merely a religious sentiment but a means to secure the highest benefit for human society.

The fully beautiful scenery after the rainy season was attractive to the eyes of everyone, including Śrī Kṛṣṇa, the cause of all causes.

28 ***The fully beautiful scenery after the rainy season was attractive to the eyes of everyone, including Śrī Kṛṣṇa, the cause of all causes.***

We should always appreciate the creative energy of the Supreme Lord. Beautiful nature, even though material and therefore temporary, is always full of the glories of the creator. There is a class of philosophers who condemn the material creation as false. They say that Brahman is truth but the creation is false. This is not good. The temporary creation is also a relative truth. It is in fact the temporary picture of the eternal creation. The forgetful soul has no information of the spiritual creation, known as the *sanātana-dhāma,* but the temporary creation gives an idea of this original creation. The devotees of the Lord, therefore, make the best use of the bad bargain by utilizing the temporary creation in the service of the Lord.

Everything emanates as different energies from the Lord, and thus everything should be engaged for His service only. As soon as even temporary things are engaged in His service, they take on permanent values. The process of such engagement in the service of the Lord is what the sages call *cikitsitam,* or 'well treated'. If we have some kind of trouble in the stomach from drinking milk, the physician prescribes the same milk in the form of yoghurt, which is nothing but treated milk. Similarly, the temporary creation of the material world is undoubtedly full of miseries, but when accepted in terms of its relation with the Supreme Lord, the whole thing becomes as well treated as the yoghurt. Everything accepted in full God consciousness has its spiritual value, and by the grace of the Almighty its material effects are diminished in terms of the increasing degree of spiritual consciousness. That is the process for cultivating the human spirit.

29 ***Thus the rainy season came to an end. The autumn began, and there were no more clouds in the sky. All the reservoirs of water became crystal clear, and the wind was no longer forceful. Lord Kṛṣṇa, along with His elder brother, Lord Baladeva, lived at Vṛndāvana in this auspicious season.***

When the sky is clear of all clouds there is no longer any distinction between the portion of the sky that was covered and that which was never covered. Similarly, when the living entity now covered by the modes of material nature is freed from ignorance, passion, and so-called goodness, he becomes one with the Absolute Truth. Such oneness is called *mukti,* or freedom from the miseries of material life. There are five different kinds of *mukti.* Impersonalists prefer to merge into the existence of the Transcendence, but the personalists, or devotees, do not annihilate their individuality, and thus the devotees of the Lord individually enjoy spiritual variegatedness on the planets of the spiritual sky.

The material sky is also the spiritual sky, but it is covered by the modes of material nature. This material nature is also a temporary creation of the Lord, as the cloud is a creation of the sun. When the cloud of the material modes is cleared off, the material nature is said to have been annihilated.

There are two kinds of living entities, namely the conditioned and the pure. It is for the conditioned living entities that the material nature is created, and the conditioned souls are put into it to become pure, unconditioned souls. Those who become unconditioned by devotional service enter into the eternal kingdom of God, and those who lose the chance rot in dormant material conditions, sometimes manifested and sometimes unmanifested. Lord Śrī Kṛṣṇa descends to reclaim the conditioned souls.

30 ***In autumn all the reservoirs of water become enriched with growing lotuses. The muddy water again becomes normally clear and decorated, just as fallen, conditioned souls once more become spiritually enriched in devotional service.***

We should not be disappointed in our muddy life of material existence, for as soon as we voluntarily take to the devotional service of the Lord our whole life becomes clear, like water in autumn. Devoid of our relationship with God our life is barren, but as soon as the muddy mind is cleared by spiritual association or cultivation of the human spirit, the threefold miseries of material life are at once cleared off. Thus the lotus of knowledge gradually fructifies, and this gradual process of development ushers in transcendental bliss.

The whole spiritual process is technically called *yoga,* or linking with the Supreme. It is something like a long staircase, and the upward steps are variously designated as regulated work, transcendental knowledge, mystic powers, and ultimately *bhakti-yoga,* or devotional service. *Bhakti-yoga* is pure and unalloyed, being entirely beyond all the preliminary steps. Such unalloyed devotional service in favour of the Supreme Lord was displayed at Vṛndāvana when the Lord descended there, and thus the *yoga* exhibited by the *gopīs* of Vṛndāvana is the highest unalloyed love of Godhead, the perfection of *bhakti-yoga.* To rise to the stage of love shown by the *gopīs* is very difficult, but this stage is attainable for serious conditioned souls.

Unfortunately, cheap neophytes make a show of the transcendental ecstasies of the *gopīs,* bringing them onto the mundane plane for perverted manifestations and thus clearing the way to hell by such unwanted caricatures. Serious students of *yoga,* however, practise it seriously, and thus they attain the highest perfection in *bhakti-yoga,* as stated in *Bhagavad-gītā* (6.47):

yoginām api sarveṣāṁ
mad-gatenāntar-ātmanā
śraddhāvān bhajate yo māṁ
sa me yuktatamo mataḥ

'And of all *yogīs,* the one with great faith who always abides in Me, thinks of Me within himself, and renders transcendental loving service to Me — he is the most intimately united with Me in *yoga* and is the highest of all. That is My opinion.'

31 ***The four prominent features of autumn are that there is no water in the sky, the weeds that grew here and there in the rainy season all wither away, the muddy roads and fields dry up, and the ponds of water become crystal clear. These four features of the autumn atmosphere are compared to the four orders of life.***

In the *varṇāśrama* system the student goes to the *āśrama* of the master to take lessons from him and serve him, even as a menial servant. The troubles of the student are at once mitigated when he attains transcendental knowledge in terms of his relation with Śrī Kṛṣṇa, the Personality of Godhead. As the white clouds no longer bear the burden of water in the autumn sky, the student finds that the troubles of drawing water for the master become a burdenless job if the student, by the grace of his master, attains to spiritual knowledge.

Householders who beget children without restriction, like weeds in the rainy season, become solitary as soon as they attain to the stage of devotional service. The family planning of a godless civilization cannot check weedlike unwanted population. People should learn to check sex life by voluntary restraint. This voluntary restraint is possible when one is dovetailed with the service of the Lord. This is confirmed in *Bhagavad-gītā.*

viṣayā vinivartante
nirāhārasya dehinaḥ
rasa-varjaṁ raso 'py asya
paraṁ dṛṣṭvā nivartate

'The embodied soul may be restricted from sense enjoyment, though the taste for sense objects remains. But, ceasing such engagements by experiencing a higher taste, he is fixed in consciousness.' (Bg. 2.59)

Well-situated devotees of the Lord refrain from materialistic sense enjoyment, for they are attracted by the beauty of the Transcendence. Forcible restraint by regulative family planning or similar artificial means cannot work very long; one must be attracted by the Transcendence. One can give up the inferior quality of enjoyment as soon as one receives the superior quality of spiritual enjoyment. So family planning is successful when one is engaged in the culture of the human spirit.

The *vānaprasthas,* who voluntarily avoid cleaning themselves and who allow their beards and nails to grow, no longer feel the discomforts of these burdens when they engage in the service of the Lord. And above all, the mendicants who take a vow to refrain from sex life no longer feel sexual urges when fixed in the transcendental service of the Lord.

Therefore, in all four spiritual orders and four grades of social life, devotional service to the Lord is essential. Without this relationship, all the regulative principles of *varṇa* and *āśrama* become burdensome duties, as they have in the age of Kali. When the regulative principles have no aim, the *varṇas* become a caste system and the *āśramas* become the business of various shopkeepers. All these anomalies of the present social system can be reformed only by cultivation of the human spirit in the devotional service of the Lord.

32 ***The beautiful white clouds, freed from all burdens of water distribution, float in midair, like mendicants freed from all family responsibilities.***

As long as one is attached to the so-called responsibilities of family burdens, he is always full of cares and anxieties about meeting his family expenses. The four orders of social life, as designed in the *varṇāśrama* system, are very scientific and cooperative. In student life one is taught the primary principles of the human form of life. One who enters the householder's life can execute the duties of a family man because he has already been trained for this job in the *brahmacarya-āśrama.* And after fifty years of age the householder retires from family life and prepares for the life of *sannyāsa.*

The householder is duty-bound to maintain the members of all three of the other *āśramas,* namely the *brahmacārīs,* the *vānaprasthas,* and *sannyāsīs.* In this way, every member of society was given a chance to retire for a higher order of spiritual culture, and the householders neglected no one. The *brahmacārīs, vānaprasthas,* and *sannyāsīs* all curtailed their necessities to the minimum, and therefore no one would begrudge maintaining them in the bare necessities of life.

In Kali-yuga, however, the entire system has gone topsy-turvy. The student lives in luxury at the expense of the father or the father-in-law. When the educated, indulgent student becomes a householder by the strength of university degrees, he requires money by all means for all kinds of bodily comfort, and therefore he cannot spare even a penny for the so-called *vānaprasthas* and *sannyāsīs*. The *vānaprasthas* and *sannyāsīs* nowadays are those who were unsuccessful in family life. Thus the so-called *sannyāsīs* try to construct another home in the name of the *sannyāsa-āśrama* and glide down into all sorts of luxury at the expense of others. So all these *varṇas* and *āśramas* have now become so many transcendental frauds.

But that does not mean that there is no reality in them. One should not conclude that there is no good money simply because one has met with counterfeit coins. The *sannyāsa-āśrama* is meant for complete freedom from all anxieties, and it is meant for uplifting the fallen souls, who are merged in materialism. But unless the *sannyāsī* is freed from all cares and anxieties, like a white cloud, it is difficult for him to do anything good for society.

33 ***There are waterfalls flowing from the hills of the forest, but sometimes water does not flow from them. So the waterfalls are not like ordinary rainfall. They are compared to great reformers, who speak or do not speak, as the time requires.***

There are two different kinds of religious preachers. One of them is called the professional preacher, and the other is called the *ācārya.* The professional preachers are like the rainfall from the sky, but the *ācāryas* are like waterfalls. The professional traders in *Bhāgavatam* and *Rāmāyaṇa* will speak from the portion of the scripture that will appeal to the mundane senses of the audience. For example, the professional *Bhāgavatam* reciter will generally speak on the subject of *rāsa-līlā,* which appears to the layman to be something like the dealings of ordinary men and women. Thus the professional reciters earn money from their so-called admirers. But an *ācārya* will never speak on *rāsa-līlā* to the general mass of people. The *rāsa-līlā* chapters of the *Bhāgavatam* are the most confidential part of the scripture, and they are meant for advanced students of spiritual realization. In the *Bhāgavatam* there are twelve cantos, and the *rāsa-līlā* is in the tenth. So before one comes to the Tenth Canto, the *Bhāgavatam* tries to convince him of the transcendental nature of the Absolute Truth. Unless one has grasped the spiritual status of the Supreme Personality of Godhead, one is sure to accept Him as an ordinary man and thereby commit offenses at His lotus feet by so many unwanted activities.

The *ācārya* is he who knows the scriptures well and teaches his disciples in terms of the disciple's capacity to understand and advance in spiritual realization. Therefore he sometimes speaks and sometimes does not speak. The holy messages of Godhead have to be received from the realized soul, and not from the professional man. Although rainwater and the waterfalls are the same, the water from the waterfalls has a different effect than ordinary rainwater. One should not accept messages from the professional men, as one should not accept milk touched by the tongue of a serpent. Milk is good, but as soon as it is touched by the snake it becomes poisonous. The *ācārya,* therefore, is not a mercenary order-supplier like the professional reciter of scriptures.

34 ***Small pools of water accumulate during the rainy season, and in the autumn they gradually dry up. The little creatures playing in those small pools do not understand that their days are now numbered and will end very soon. Thus they are like foolish men who, not caring for the nearing day of their death, become absorbed in the so-called enjoyment of family life.***

Foolish politicians are too attached to family life. A big politician means a big family man. An ordinary family man is attached to his limited family of wife and children, but big politicians extend the same family feeling to a wider circle and thus become encumbered by false prestige, honour, and self-interest. The politician never retires from politics, even if he has enjoyed many covetable posts, like those of minister or president. The older he is, the more he is attached to his false prestige. Even at the fag end of his life he thinks that everything will be spoiled without him. He is so foolish that he does not see that many other politicians who thought like him have come and gone, with no gain or loss for want of them. These family men, big and small, are like the small fish in the pools of water that gradually dry up in the autumn. They are foolish because they think that their attachment to their family, even at the end of their lives, will be able to protect them from the cruel hands of death.

As already mentioned, the human life must be divided into four component parts: the student life, the householder life, the preparative life, and the life of dedication to the service of the Lord. One must retire from all sorts of family life, big or small, at the age of fifty, and thus prepare for the next life. That is the process of human culture. The householders are allowed a pension from service so that they can live for a higher cultural life. But foolish men, reluctant even to accept this pension, want to artificially increase the duration of their life. Such foolish men should take lessons from the drying pools of water and should know, in their own interests, that life is eternal, continuing even after death. Only the body changes, whether spiritually or materially. An intelligent man should be careful to know what sort of body is going to be awarded him, and thus he must prepare for a better life in other planets, even if he is reluctant to go back to Godhead.

35 ***When the small pools of water become too hot because of the scorching heat of the autumn sun, the poor, small creatures, with their many family members, suffer terribly, as poor householders with too many family members suffer economic strains and yet go on begetting children because of uncontrolled senses.***

Human life is meant for controlling the senses, for uncontrolled senses are the cause of material bondage. But for fools sense enjoyment is the pivot of life's activities. All men undergo hard, laborious duties all day and night and in all seasons of the year, only for the sake of sense pleasure with their mates. These foolish creatures have no information of other enjoyment. In a godless civilization especially, sense pleasure, accepted in the name of culture and philosophy, is all in all. Men who are addicted to this pleasure are called *kṛpaṇas.*

When the *kṛpaṇas* have too many children, they suffer the scorching heat of family life, and then similar leaders advise them to undertake family planning. The idea of this family planning is that sense pleasure should not be curtailed, but birth control should be accomplished by artificial measures. Such methods of birth control are called *bhrūṇa-hatyā,* or killing the child in embryo. Such killing is a sinful act, and in the revealed scriptures a specific hell is designated for those who commit such sins.

Spiritual culture means pursuing a better engagement in life. When a man engages in such cultural life, the desire for mating automatically abates, and the sufferings of uncontrolled family life are mitigated without artificial means.

The attention of a human being, therefore, should be drawn to the cultivation of the human spirit, for this will gradually protect him from all sorts of discomfiture and elevate him to a higher status of life for real and eternal enjoyment in personal contact with the Personality of Godhead, Śrī Kṛṣṇa.

36 ***With the progress of the autumn season the moist earth and muddy places begin to dry up, and the green vegetation begins to fade. This drying up and fading resembles the gradual disappearance of the false sense of affinity and ego.***

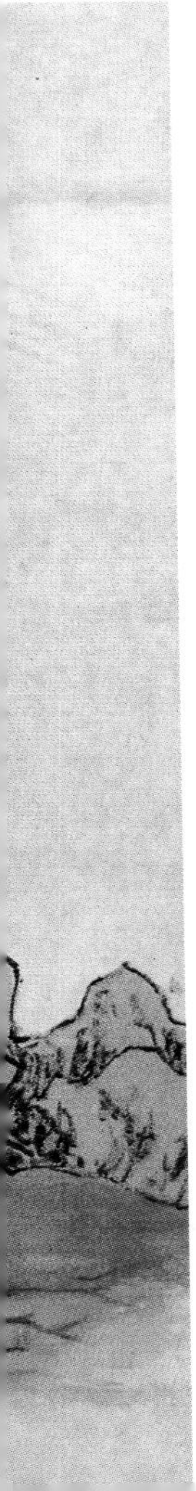

Progress in cultivating the human spirit entails the gradual disappearance of the materialistic ego. Covered by ignorance, passion, and so-called goodness, the spirit soul thinks himself all in all and is covered by a false sense of ego. Thus he falsely identifies the soul with the body, and his bodily relations with material things become the objects of his attraction. This false identification and attraction for matter gradually dry up and fade away by success in the cultivation of the human spirit. That is the effect of such higher cultivation. Progress in spiritual culture brings about the disintegration of false ego and material attraction.

The ultimate goal of cultivating the human spirit is God realization and surrender unto God with a full sense of His all-pervasive nature. When a liberated soul thus surrenders unto the lotus feet of the all-pervading Godhead, the ocean of nescience becomes as insignificant to him as the water in the small hoofprint of a calf. He at once becomes eligible to be promoted to the spiritual kingdom, and he has nothing to do with the miserable land of the material world.

Cultivation of the human spirit is not, therefore, mere adjustment of materialistic anomalies. It is the process for preparing oneself to be promoted to the spiritual kingdom. No one can adjust the sufferings of material existence, but by spiritual culture one can elevate himself from the effects of such miserable life. As an example one may cite the condition of a dry coconut. The dry coconut pulp automatically becomes separated from its outer skin. Similarly, the outer skin, or the gross and subtle material coverings of the soul, automatically separates from the spirit soul, and the spirit soul can then exist in spiritual existence, even though apparently within the dry skin. This freedom from the false sense of ego is called the liberation of the soul.

37 ***With the inauguration of the autumn season the rough sea becomes calm and quiet, just like a philosopher after self-realization, who is no longer troubled by the modes of nature.***

The result of self-realization is cessation of the storms of desire and lust, which are products of the modes of ignorance and passion. This cessation of the storm does not mean that the sea becomes inactive. When the storm subsides, the work of navigation can take place smoothly. According to the Indian system of navigation, there is a ceremony on the seashore known as the coconut day. On the coconut day the sea is offered a coconut because she has become peaceful, and from that day on, the seagoing vessels sail to foreign countries.

The three modes of nature divide human activities into two different spheres, one external and the other introspective. As long as a man is dominated by the modes of ignorance and passion, he is active externally in desire and lust. Men absorbed in desire and lust are called *asuras,* and they are always chasing after women and money. For the sake of women and money the *asuras* exploit every source of economic development. As a result of this asuric civilization, the entire human society becomes like a stormy sea, with no trace of peace and prosperity.

Too much of an external view of the world gives rise to an overly large-scale and difficult type of industry and trade, known as *ugra-karma.* The word *ugra* means 'hard' or 'difficult', and *karma* means 'task'. The development of hard and difficult industrial undertakings always hinders the progressive cultivation of the human spirit. Asuric leaders of society never retire from such lustful undertakings unless killed by the laws of nature. For them there is no question of retirement or of cultivating the human spirit. But men in the mode of goodness have an introspective mind, and after a regulative struggle for existence they retire at a ripe old age and engage their time in cultivating the human spirit.

According to the *varṇāśrama* principle, it is compulsory that one retire after the age of fifty, without considering other circumstances. Business offices close at a fixed hour no matter what balance of work remains. Similarly, after the age of fifty one must retire from the active, external life and devote oneself to the introspective cultivation of the human spirit. This retirement must be compulsory, so that foolish old men will no longer disturb the peaceful progress of spiritual culture. In the modern democratic government, no one should be elected after the age of fifty. Otherwise the storm of the ocean of nescience cannot be stopped to allow the ships and boats to sail back to Godhead. The greatest enemies of progressive spiritual culture in human society are the old fossils of political parties who are blind themselves and who try to lead other blind men. They bring about disaster in a peaceful human society. The members of the younger generation are not as stupid as the old politicians, and therefore by state law the foolish old politicians must retire from active life at the age of fifty.

38 ***After the rainy season, the farmers begin to rebuild the partitioning walls of the paddy fields so that the water will be conserved, just as yogīs try to use their conserved energy for self-realization.***

The living being is the marginal energy of the Absolute Personality of Godhead, and he can spend his conserved energy either externally or internally. When spent internally, the energy is identified with the internal energy of the Personality of Godhead, but the same conserved energy, when spent for His external energy, is identified with that external energy. All energies — internal, external, and marginal — are emanations from Him, the Supreme, and they act differently to prove diversity in unity. The unity is the Lord, and the energies represent diversity. The Lord is so powerful that He can do anything and everything merely by His sweet will alone. As mentioned above, everything is done by His energies in a natural way, with full knowledge and complete perfection. That is the information we have from the Vedic literatures.

The internal energy and the marginal energy are of the same superior quality, but the external energy is inferior in quality. That is the information we have from *Bhagavad-gītā*. Because the living entity is classified as marginal energy and is of the same quality as the internal energy, it is quite natural for him to cooperate with the internal energy. But when the living entity prefers to cooperate with the external energy, he is put into difficulty. By the process called *pratyāhāra* (diversion), *yoga* diverts our energies from the external to the internal.

The energy of our senses is meant to be diverted, not stopped. The senses are to be purified, so that they serve the Lord instead of disturbing His settled harmony. The entire cosmic harmony is a settled fact by the will of the Supreme. So we must find the supreme will in every action of the cosmic situation. That is the instruction of *Īśopaniṣad*. The human life is an opportunity to understand this cosmic harmony, and therefore our conserved energy, which is likened to the conserved water in the paddy field, must be used for this purpose only.

As there is no chance of rain from the sky in autumn, we shall not immediately have a chance to get a human body again if we spend our conserved energy for sense enjoyment. The senses have their utility for the service of the Lord, and if properly engaged they can reach the highest perfection by being directly engaged in the service of the Lord in His personal presence. When the living entity thus goes back home, back to Godhead, and engages in the personal service of the Lord, he is said to have attained *saṁsiddhi paramā*, the highest perfection. This is confirmed in the *Bhagavad-gītā*.

mām upetya punar janma
duḥkhālayam aśāśvatam
nāpnuvanti mahātmānaḥ
saṁsiddhiṁ paramāṁ gatāḥ

'After attaining Me, the great souls, who are *yogīs* in devotion, never return to this temporary world, which is full of miseries, because they have attained the highest perfection.' (Bg. 8.15)

39 *In the autumn there is a gulf of difference between the day and the night. During the day the extreme heat of the sun is unbearable, but at night the moonlight is extremely soothing and refreshing. Similarly, Lord Śrī Kṛṣṇa is soothing for both the gopīs and the mundane man in illusion, who accepts the body as the soul.*

As long as the living being, under illusion, accepts the body or the mind as the soul, he will always be unhappy, like a man in the burning heat of autumn. But when the same living being becomes a devotee of Lord Śrī Kṛṣṇa, the Personality of Godhead, he at once lives a soothing life, as if under the cooling rays of the moon in autumn. Lord Śrī Kṛṣṇa is so merciful that He descends to reclaim suffering humanity and preaches *Bhagavad-gītā* with the intense desire that all living beings give up all of their engagements and take shelter of His lotus feet. This is the most confidential part of all revealed scripture.

The example of the damsels of Vrajabhūmi Vṛndāvana (the *gopīs*) is given here because these eternal consorts of the Lord terribly suffered the separation of Lord Kṛṣṇa when the Lord was absent from their presence for His engagement in tending the cows in the forest. During the absence of Kṛṣṇa, the entire day would appear to the *gopīs* to be as unbearable as a hot day in autumn. The Lord so much appreciated this natural feeling of the *gopīs* that He declared His inability to repay their intense love. Lord Caitanya recommended the feeling of the *gopīs* as the highest mode of worship that can be rendered to the Lord. The conclusion is that the regular practice of *bhakti-yoga* will lead the devotee to the plane of intense love for the Lord, and that is the single qualification by which the conditioned soul is allowed to reenter the eternal life of bliss in the kingdom of God. The threefold miseries of material existence are at once nullified by intense love of God, which is the ultimate goal of cultivating the human spirit.

40 ***In the clear autumn sky the twinkling stars appear brighter and brighter, just like a transcendentalist with clear vision of the purpose of the Vedas.***

It is said that the import of the *Vedas* becomes clear to one who is not only a sincere devotee of the Lord but also a sincere servitor of the spiritual master. The spiritual master knows the purpose of the *Vedas,* practises it personally, and teaches the disciple of the true light of the *Vedas.* The supreme spiritual master, Lord Śrī Kṛṣṇa, teaches us the import of the *Vedas* in the following verse of *Bhagavad-gītā* (15.16):

dvāv imau puruṣau loke
kṣaraś cākṣara eva ca
kṣaraḥ sarvāṇi bhūtāni
kūṭa-stho 'kṣara ucyate

'There are two classes of beings, the fallible and the infallible. In the material world every living entity is fallible, and in the spiritual world every living entity is called infallible.'

The Lord says that in the *Vedas* it is mentioned that there are two kinds of living beings, called the fallible and the infallible. Those living beings who are materially encaged are all fallible, whereas those who are not conditioned and who are eternally situated in the spiritual realm are called *akṣara,* or infallible. The Lord then says,

uttamaḥ puruṣas tv anyaḥ
paramātmety udāhṛtaḥ
yo loka-trayam āviśya
bibharty avyaya īśvaraḥ

'Besides these two, there is the greatest living personality, the Supreme Soul, the imperishable Lord Himself, who has entered the three worlds and is maintaining them.' (Bg. 15.17)

yasmāt kṣaram atīto 'ham
akṣarād api cottamaḥ
ato 'smi loke vede ca
prathitaḥ puruṣottamaḥà

'Because I am transcendental, beyond both the fallible and the infallible, and because I am the greatest, I am celebrated both in the world and the *Vedas* as that Supreme Person.' (Bg. 15.18)

The import of the *Vedas* is still more explicitly explained in *Śrīmad-Bhāgavatam.* The conclusion of the Vedic literatures is that Lord Śrī Kṛṣṇa is the primeval Lord and the cause of all causes. He has His eternal two-armed form as Śyāmasundara, with features exactly like those of a most beautiful young man, and that is the sum and substance of the *Vedas* concerning God. God is one, but the living entities, including both the liberated and the conditioned, are many and have many different grades of positions. The living entities are never equal to God, but as parts and parcels of the Lord they are eternally His servitors. As long as the living entities are situated normally as His servitors they are happy; otherwise they are always unhappy. That is the Vedic conclusion.

41 ***In the clear sky of autumn, the beautiful moon among the beautiful stars becomes the cynosure of all eyes, just as Lord Śrī Kṛṣṇa is the central attraction in the Vṛṣṇi dynasty or in the family of Yadu.***

The Personality of Godhead, Śrī Kṛṣṇa, appeared in the family of Yadu, and since then the Yadu dynasty has been luminous like the moon in autumn. The appearance and disappearance of the Lord are similar to the appearance and disappearance of the sun. The sun is first seen on the eastern horizon, but that does not mean that the sun is the son of that side. The sun is fixed in its own orbit, and it neither rises nor sets. But because we first see it on the eastern horizon we may say that the sun rises on that side. Similarly, the appearance of Godhead in some particular family does not mean that He is limited by obligations to that family. He is fully independent and may appear and disappear anywhere and everywhere, because He is all-pervading.

Less intelligent persons cannot accommodate the appearance and disappearance of the Lord as an incarnation, but there is no sound reasoning to support such unbelievers. If God is all-pervading, like the power of electricity, He can manifest Himself at any place within His creation. When He is within we cannot see Him, but when He is without He is seen by everyone, although very few know Him as He is. Everyone sees the sun every day, but that does not mean that everyone knows what the sun actually is. Similarly, when Lord Śrī Kṛṣṇa was present five thousand years ago, very few could know what He was.

Anyone who comes to know Him as He is becomes liberated at once, and while leaving this present body such a knower goes back to Godhead, never to return to this universe of manifold miseries. In *Bhagavad-gītā* (4.9) the Lord confirms this as follows:

janma karma ca me divyam
evaṁ yo vetti tattvataḥ
tyaktvā dehaṁ punar janma
naiti mām eti so 'rjuna

'My birth and activities are all transcendental. One who knows them in reality will not be conditioned by another material body but will come back to My abode, where there is no birth and death.'

But there are foolish persons who take Him to be an ordinary man, not knowing the essence of His transcendental features. In *Bhagavad-gītā* (9.11) the Lord affirms this:

avajānanti māṁ mūḍhā
mānuṣīṁ tanum āśritam
paraṁ bhāvam ajānanto
mama bhūta-maheśvaram

'Fools deride Me when I descend in the human form. They do not know My transcendental nature as the Supreme Lord of all that be.'

***42** At night in autumn the atmosphere is pleasant because it is neither very hot nor very cold. The mild wind blowing through the gardens of fruits and flowers in Vṛndāvana appeared very much pleasing to all — all but the gopīs, who were always overtaken by heartfelt sorrow in the absence of Kṛṣṇa.*

There are two kinds of transcendental feelings for those engaged in the worship of the Lord. One is called *sambhoga,* and the other is called *viraha.* According to authorities in the disciplic line, *viraha* worship is more palatable than *sambhoga* worship. *Sambhoga* takes place in direct touch, whereas *viraha* takes place without such direct contact. Lord Caitanya Mahāprabhu taught us to accept *viraha* worship. In the present state of affairs we cannot make any direct touch with the Personality of Godhead. But if we practise the *viraha* mode of worship we can transcendentally realize the presence of the Lord more lovingly than in His presence.

Without love of Godhead there is no meaning even to direct contact. During the presence of the Lord there were thousands and thousands of men, but because they were not in love of Godhead they could hardly realize the Personality of Godhead, Śrī Kṛṣṇa. Therefore we must first activate our dormant love of Godhead by following the prescribed rules and by following in the footsteps of the authorities who are actually fixed in love of Godhead. The *gopīs* provide the highest example of such unalloyed love of Godhead, and Lord Caitanya at the ultimate stage of realization displayed the *viraha* worship in the mood of the *gopīs.*

In the mundane world there is also some shadow of such *viraha*. A loving wife, husband, or friend may for some time be maddened by the absence of the beloved. Such a state of mind, however, is not permanent. The loving husband or wife takes to another and forgets everything of the past. This is so because there is no reality to such relationships in the material world.

The spiritual situation, however, is completely different. A bona fide lover of God could never forget Him, even in exchange for everything else. The devotee of the Lord cannot be happy in any circumstance without the Lord. In the absence of the Lord the devotee associates with Him by remembering His separation, and because the Lord is absolute, the devotee's feeling of separation is transcendentally more relishable than direct contact. This is possible only when we develop genuine love for Him. In that state the devotee is always with the Lord by feelings of separation, which become more acute and intolerable in suitable circumstances. The mild wind reminded the *gopīs* of the association of the Lord, and they felt separation from Him acutely.

43 ***In the autumn season all the birds, beasts, and men become sexually disposed, and the bull, the stag, the male bird, the man, and other male creatures forcibly impregnate the fair sex. A similar impregnation takes place as a result of devotional service to the Lord.***

Devotional service to the Lord never goes in vain. Just at the right moment, the result of one's particular devotional service will come, even if one has no desire for it. The pure devotees do not wish any return from the Lord in exchange for their service; they do not make business exchanges with the Lord. But the Lord, out of His own accord, fulfills all the desires of the devotees.

It may appear that a devotee of the Lord is becoming poorer and poorer in terms of material prosperity, but factually he is not. The typical example is the Pāṇḍavas. The five brothers, headed by King Yudhiṣṭhira, underwent all sorts of difficulties because of the conspiracy of their cousins, headed by Duryodhana. But in the long run King Yudhiṣṭhira was enthroned by Lord Śrī Kṛṣṇa, and his enemies were vanquished. King Yudhiṣṭhira was never disturbed by all the calamities that overcame them even though Lord Kṛṣṇa was ever their companion. The Pāṇḍavas never prayed to the Lord for anything but His devotional service, and in due time everything came out in favour of the devotees.

A devotee, therefore, should execute his devotional services with full energy, endurance, and confidence. He should perform his scheduled duties, he should be pure in heart, and he should serve in association with devotees. All six of these items will lead the devotee to the path of success. One should not be discouraged in the discharge of devotional service. Failures may not be detrimental; they may be the pillars of success. One must have good faith in the regulative principles followed by the self-realized souls, and one should not be doubtful about the ultimate result of such devotional service. Rather, one must go on executing his prescribed duties without hesitation, and one should never be influenced by unwanted association.

We should not consider going back to Godhead a plaything. We must take it seriously, as enjoined in the scriptures. For a strict follower, the result is sure and certain, and when the time is right the result will come of its own force. Dhruva Mahārāja went to worship God to gain something, but when he actually came in contact with God he did not want anything from the Lord. The Lord, however, awarded Dhruva Mahārāja both benefits — that is, the Lord fulfilled his desires and also gave him eternal salvation. Such are the lessons we learn from all the revealed scriptures. The almighty God awards the results we desire, and therefore we should desire that which is eternal, blissful, and full of knowledge. In devotional service we should not endeavour for that which is temporary and useless.

***44** In the autumn season all the reservoirs of water are full of lotus flowers. There are also flowers that resemble the lotus but are of a different class. Among them is a flower called kumuda. When the sun rises, all the flowers but the kumuda blossom beautifully. Similarly, lotuslike men take pleasure in the advent of a responsible king, but men who are like the kumuda do not like the existence of a king.*

In this age of Kali the people want their own government, because the kings have become corrupt. Formerly it was not like that. The sons of kings were trained under the guidance of a good *brāhmaṇa-ācārya* just as the Pāṇḍavas and the Kauravas were put under the instruction of the qualified *brāhmaṇa* professor Śrī Droṇācārya. Princes were rigidly trained in politics, economics, the military arts, ethics and morality, the sciences, and, above all, devotional service to the Lord. Only after such good training were the princes allowed to be enthroned. When such a prince became king, then too he was guided by the advice of good *brāhmaṇas.* Even in the Middle Ages, Mahārāja Candragupta was guided by the learned *brāhmaṇa* Cāṇakya Paṇḍita.

In a monarchy, one man sufficiently trained was competent enough to conduct alone the business of the state. But in a democracy no one is trained like a prince; instead, politicians are voted to responsible posts of administration by diplomatic arrangements. In place of one king or supreme executive officer, in a democracy there are so many quasi kings: the president, the ministers, the deputy ministers, the secretaries, the assistant secretaries, the private secretaries, and the undersecretaries. There are a number of parties — political, social, and communal — and there are party whips, party whims, and so on. But no one is well enough trained to look after the factual interests of the governed. In a so-called democratic government, corruption is even more rampant than in an autocracy or monarchy.

Men who want to flourish in the guise of servants of the people do not want a good king at the head of the state. They are like the *kumuda* flowers, which do not take pleasure in the sunrise. The word *ku* means 'bad', and *mud* means 'pleasure'. Persons who want to exploit the administrative power for their own self-interest do not like the presence of a good king. Although professing democracy, they want to be kings themselves. Thus they compete for votes by bad propaganda and take pleasure in having politics but no king. Thieves and dacoits also take no pleasure in the presence of a good king, but it is in the interest of the people to have a well-trained king as the head of the state.

45 ***After the new grains were cut and brought home from the paddy fields, the people began to observe the navānna ceremony everywhere, in the presence of the Lord as Śrī Kṛṣṇa and Baladeva.***

According to Vedic culture, learned men consider all natural products, such as food grains, fruits, flowers, and milk, to be God-sent. No one can manufacture these things in man-made factories, however scientifically advanced people may be. People can make preparations of such God-sent foodstuffs, but they cannot manufacture the natural ingredients. Spiritually cultured men, therefore, feel obliged to the Lord when they get sufficient natural foodstuffs by the grace of the Lord.

The *navānna-prāśana* ceremony is observed as a way of acknowledging the gifts of God. Newly collected grains would first be offered to the Lord by the villagers, either individually or collectively, and in either case all the members of the village would partake of the *prasādam* thus offered to the Lord. Such ceremonies make the people happy and prosperous.

We should always acknowledge the mercy of God. We should not think that we can produce ample food grains merely with the help of tractors and fertilizers. These can help us only as instruments for such production; without the sanction of the Lord there is no possibility of having grains, even if there are trucks and fertilizers.

When Lord Kṛṣṇa and Baladeva were present, the good men of Vṛndāvana realized that it was due to the presence of the Lord that their supply of food grains was sufficient. Some of the people of Vṛndāvana, including Lord Kṛṣṇa's father, Nanda Mahārāja, used to perform sacrifices to propitiate King Indra, the king of heaven, because he is the controller of rains. Without good rains, grains cannot be produced, and therefore the people would offer sacrifices to Indra. Lord Śrī Kṛṣṇa, however, stopped this age-old ceremony and advised His father to offer the same sacrifice to the Supreme Lord. His purpose was to teach that we need not satisfy the various demigods in charge of the various departments of cosmic affairs; instead we must offer sacrifices to the Supreme Lord, for the Lord is the master and all others are His servants. The famous *anna-kūṭa* ceremony, performed in Vṛndāvana especially and also in all other parts of India, was thus introduced by the Lord, and people still follow this path by worshiping Govardhana Hill, where the Lord used to take pleasure in tending cows. People also worship Giri Govardhana as identical with the Lord, because there is no difference between God and His paraphernalia and pastimes.

46 ***The merchants, preachers, kings, and students who were confined to home during the four months June, July, August, and September began to flow out and attain success in life, just as perfected souls attain the required body as soon as they leave the present one.***

The people in general — especially the merchants, preachers, kings, and students — are advised not to leave home during the four months of the rainy season. These four months are known as Cāturmāsya, and for everyone there are specific rules for observing this period, partly for the sake of health and partly for spiritual realization. During this period the merchants cannot do free business, dedicated souls like *sannyāsīs* cannot freely preach the doctrines of the *Vedas,* kings cannot go out to tour their states, and students cannot go to their schools, which are closed. But after the Cāturmāsya period they all get the freedom to go out and perform their respective duties, and by doing so they can achieve the results they desire.

In the same way, one cannot achieve the desired results of one's penances until one attains freedom from the present body. There are various ways to practise the various kinds of *yoga* to attain various results in various spheres of life. It is not that everything is the same. There are varieties of life, varieties of planets, and varieties of success in spiritual realization. And all these can be achieved only when we have finished the Cāturmāsya-like period of life. It is a foolish imagination, therefore, that we can go to other planets in the present body. If we want to go to Devaloka, the planets of the demigods, we must achieve the required qualifications, and the same is true if we want to go back to the kingdom of God. If we want to remain on this planet in some better condition of life, that also will depend on the required achievements. In any case, those achievements can be fulfilled just after one leaves the body.

The merchants, preachers, kings, and students form the four important sections of human society. The merchants should see that everyone gets his proper share of the food given as a gift by God. The *sannyāsī* preachers should go from door to door to preach the sense of God consciousness, not to build *maṭhas* and temples but to enlighten the people. The king should go out from his home to see with his own eyes how things are going on. (Mahārāja Parīkṣit, while on tour, saw a man, Kali, attempting to kill a cow, so the king at once punished him.) And students should gather knowledge wherever it is available. The combined work of these four sections is meant for the general welfare of society.

47 ***From the Transcendence, which is called Kṛṣṇaloka, there emanates a glowing effulgence that resembles the tail of a comet. This glowing effulgence is unlimited, immeasurable, and unfathomable. Within this effulgence there are innumerable glowing planets, each of them self-luminous. Somewhere, a limited part of that glowing effulgence is covered by material energy, just as a part of the sky is covered by a cloud. Within this material energy there are innumerable universes, in every universe there are innumerable material planets, and the earth is one of these planets. Thus we can understand what an insignificant part of the entire cosmos is this globe on which we live.***

Kṛṣṇaloka, as above mentioned, is the residence of the Personality of Godhead, the original Transcendence. The glowing effulgence emanating from Kṛṣṇaloka is the personal glow of the Lord. The almighty Lord, being full of inconceivable energies, expands Himself in various forms and energies. There are forms from His energy as well as forms from His person. He has innumerable energies, and therefore He can do anything and everything as He desires, and these things take place immediately, with all perfection. His energies are like the heat and light that expand from a fire. The entire cosmic manifestation is nothing but an expansion of His energies; the energies are emanations from Him, and therefore the emanations are simultaneously one with and different from Him.

The Transcendence is compared to milk, and the emanations are compared to yoghurt. Yoghurt is nothing but milk, but at the same time it is different from milk. Yoghurt is a milk preparation, but it cannot be used in place of milk. The Lord is also sometimes compared to a tree. The root of the tree is the cause of the trunk, branches, twigs, leaves, and fruits, yet the trunk is not the fruit, the fruit is not the leaf, nor is the leaf the root. When water is needed it has to be poured on the root, not on the leaves. Pouring water on the leaves serves no purpose, but pouring water on the root serves all purposes. This is the essence of the philosophy of spiritual culture.

Kṛṣṇaloka is also called Goloka Vṛndāvana. Beneath this Goloka are Hari-dhāma, Maheśa-dhāma, and Devī-dhāma. Hari (Viṣṇu, Nārāyaṇa) is the formal expansion of the Lord; Maheśa (Śiva) is the formal energetic expansion of the Lord; and Devī is the Lord's energetic expansion. The living entities are also energetic expansions of the Lord. There are two different kinds of living entities, called the liberated souls and the conditioned souls.

The planets within the glowing effulgence are called Hari-dhāma. On these planets the predominating Deity is Hari, and the predominated deities are the liberated souls. The features of the liberated souls and those of Hari are almost the same, yet Hari is predominator and the liberated souls are predominated. The innumerable planets in Hari-dhāma are predominated by different formal expansions of the Lord, and all of them have different names.

The universes within the material energy are called Devī-dhāma, and within Devī-dhāma the predominating Deity is Viṣṇu, who is assisted by Brahmā and Śiva. Devī-dhāma is controlled by three modes, namely goodness, passion, and ignorance. Viṣṇu is the incarnation of goodness, Brahmā of passion, and Śiva of ignorance. Brahmā creates, Viṣṇu maintains, and Śiva destroys the material creation. The material creation comes into being by the will of the Lord, and it is again annihilated by His will. But although the universes of the material energy are thus created and annihilated, the planets in Hari-dhāma are ever existent.

The conditioned living entities who wish to enjoy and not serve are given a chance within Devī-dhāma to seek liberation. Some of them enter Hari-dhāma, some of them enter Maheśa-dhāma, and some of them remain within Devī-dhāma. Maheśa-dhāma is the marginal place between Hari-dhāma and Devī-dhāma. The impersonalists who want to merge into the existence of the Transcendence are placed within Maheśa-dhāma. Those who want to remain within the planetary systems of the material universes do so on various planets. But those who want to go outside the material energy can enter Hari-dhāma and go either to the various planets there or directly to Kṛṣṇaloka.

The system of *bhakti-yoga* makes one eligible to enter Hari-dhāma, the system of *jñāna-yoga* makes one eligible to enter Maheśa-dhāma, and the system of *karma-yoga* obliges one to remain in Devī-dhāma and repeatedly be born and die, changing his material covering according to the standard of *karma* he performs.

***48** The moon, or Candraloka, is one of the four important places of residence for the demigods. Beyond Mānasa Lake is Sumeru Mountain. On the eastern side of this mountain is the planet Devadhānī, where Indra resides. On the southern side is the planet known as Saṁyamanī, where Yamarāja resides. On the western side is the planet known as Nimlocanī, the residence of Vāyu, the demigod who controls the wind. And on the northern side of the mountain is the moon, which is also known as Vibhāvarī.*

All these various planets are within the universe in which our planet is situated. Persons who are too materialistic always engage in sense enjoyment. Such persons worship the material demigods and goddesses to fulfill their material desires. They are fond of performing many *yajñas* to propitiate the various demigods and the forefathers in heaven. Such persons are automatically promoted to the moon, where they enjoy *soma,* a celestial beverage.

The moon is too cold for the inhabitants of this earth, and therefore ordinary persons who want to go there with earthly bodies are attempting to do so in vain. Merely seeing the moon from a distance cannot enable one to understand the real situation of the moon. One has to cross Mānasa Lake and then Sumeru Mountain, and only then can one trace out the orbit of the moon. Besides that, no ordinary man is allowed to enter that planet. Even those admitted there after death must have performed the prescribed duties to satisfy the *pitās* and *devas.* Yet even they are sent back to earth after a fixed duration of life on the moon.

Men with developed consciousness, therefore, do not waste time making excursions, real or imaginary, to the moon. Such intelligent persons do not endeavour to achieve temporary sense enjoyment. Rather, they apply their conserved energy for the sake of spiritual cultivation. They discharge religious duties for the satisfaction of the Supreme Lord and not for personal sense enjoyment. The signs of such exceptional devotees of the Lord are that they are unattached to material enjoyment, contented, pure in heart, attached to devotional service, free from affection for temporary things, and devoid of false ego. According to Vedic injunctions, such great personalities ultimately attain the place where the Supreme Personality of Godhead predominates and where there is no death, no birth, no old age, and no disease. On the way to these spiritual planets, such personalities pass through the sun line called *arcir-mārga.* And on the way they can see all the planets between here and the spiritual world.

Appendix

The Author

His Divine Grace A. C. Bhaktivedanta Swami Prabhupāda appeared in this world in 1896 in Calcutta, India. He first met his spiritual master, Śrīla Bhaktisiddhānta Sarasvatī Gosvāmī, in Calcutta in 1922. Bhaktisiddhānta Sarasvatī was a prominent religious scholar and the founder of the Gauḍīya Maṭha (a Vaiṣṇava movement with sixty-four centres) in India. He liked this educated young man and convinced him to dedicate his life to teaching Vedic knowledge. Śrīla Prabhupāda became his student and, in 1933, received initiation as his disciple.

At their first meeting, Śrīla Bhaktisiddhānta Sarasvatī requested Śrīla Prabhupāda to broadcast Vedic knowledge in English. In the years that followed, Śrīla Prabhupāda wrote a commentary on the *Bhagavad-gītā* and assisted the Gauḍīya Maṭha in its work. In 1944, he started *Back to Godhead,* a fortnightly magazine in English. Singlehandedly, Śrīla Prabhupāda edited it, typed the manuscripts, checked the galley proofs, and even distributed the individual copies. The magazine now continues to be published by his disciples throughout the world in different languages.

In 1950, Śrīla Prabhupāda retired from domestic life to devote more time to his studies and writing. He traveled to the holy town of Vṛndāvana, where he lived in humble circumstances in the historic temple of Rādhā-Dāmodara. There, for several years, he engaged in deep study and writing. He accepted the renounced order of life (*sannyāsa*) in 1959. It was at the Rādhā-Dāmodara temple that Śrīla Prabhupāda began to work on his life's masterpiece: a multivolume translation of the eighteen-thousand-verse *Śrīmad-Bhāgavatam* (*Bhāgavata Purāṇa*) with full commentary. After publishing three volumes of the *Bhāgavatam,* Śrīla Prabhupāda traveled by freighter to New York City. He was practically penniless, but he had faith that the mission of his spiritual master could be successful. On the day he landed in America and saw the grey mists hanging over the towering skyscrapers, he penned these words in his diary: 'My dear Lord Kṛṣṇa, I am sure that when this transcendental message penetrates their hearts, they will certainly feel gladdened and thus become liberated from all unhappy conditions of life.' He was sixty-nine years old, alone and with few resources, but the wealth of spiritual knowledge and devotion he possessed was an unwavering source of strength and inspiration.

'At a very advanced age, when most people would be resting on their laurels', writes Harvey Cox, Harvard University theologian and author, 'Śrīla Prabhupāda harkened to the mandate of his own spiritual teacher and set out on the difficult and demanding voyage to America. Śrīla Prabhupāda is, of course, only one of thousands of teachers. But in another sense, he is one in a thousand, maybe one in a million.'

In 1966, Śrīla Prabhupāda founded the International Society for Krishna Consciousness, which became the formal name for the Hare Kṛṣṇa Movement.

In the years that followed, Śrīla Prabhupāda gradually attracted tens of thousands of followers, started more than a hundred temples and *āśramas,* and published scores of books. His achievement is remarkable in that he transplanted India's ancient spiritual culture to the twentieth-century Western world.

In 1968, Śrīla Prabhupāda sent three devotee couples to bring Kṛṣṇa consciousness to the U.K. At first, these devotees were cared for by Hindu families who appreciated their mission, but soon they became well known in London for the public chanting in Oxford Street. A headline in the *Times* announced, 'Kṛṣṇa Chant Startles London'. But the *mahā-mantra* soon became popular. Former Beatle George Harrison, who had known Śrīla Prabhupāda and the chanting before the devotees came to England, wanted to help. He arranged to produce a recording of the *mantra* on the Beatles' Apple label. It reached the Top Ten in Britain and number one in some other countries.

When Śrīla Prabhupāda arrived in England, he was the guest of John Lennon at his estate in Tittenhurst, while work was progressing on the temple in Bloomsbury, near the British Museum. In November 1969, Śrīla Prabhupāda opened the temple — the first Rādhā-Kṛṣṇa temple in Europe. The movement grew from strength to strength. Once again, George Harrison offered to help by donating a beautiful mock-Tudor manor house and estate in Hertfordshire. Now named Bhaktivedanta Manor, it is the Society's main training centre in Britain.

New devotees of Kṛṣṇa soon became highly visible in all the major cities around the world by their public chanting and their distribution of Śrīla Prabhupāda's books of Vedic knowledge. They began staging joyous cultural festivals throughout the year and serving millions of plates of delicious food offered to Kṛṣṇa (known as *prasādam*) throughout the world. As a result, ISKCON has significantly influenced the lives of hundreds of thousands of people. The late A. L. Basham, one of the world's leading authorities on Indian history and culture, wrote, 'The Hare Kṛṣṇa movement arose out of next to nothing in less than twenty years and has become known all over the West. This is an important fact in the history of the Western world.'

In just twelve years, despite his advanced age, Śrīla Prabhupāda circled the globe fourteen times on lecture tours that took him to six continents. Yet this vigorous schedule did not slow his prolific literary output. His writings constitute a veritable library of Vedic philosophy, religion, literature, and culture.

Indeed, Śrīla Prabhupāda's most significant contribution is his books. Highly respected by academics for their authority, depth, and clarity, they are used as textbooks in numerous university courses.

Garry Gelade, a professor at Oxford University's Department of Philosophy, wrote of them: 'These texts are to be treasured. No one of whatever faith or philosophical persuasion who reads these books with an open mind can fail to be moved and impressed.' And Dr. Larry Shinn, Dean of the College of Arts and Sciences at Bucknell University, wrote, 'Prabhupāda's personal piety gave him real authority. He exhibited complete command of the scriptures, an unusual depth of realization and an outstanding personal example, because he actually lived what he taught.'

His writings have been translated into over 80 languages. The Bhaktivedanta Book Trust, established in 1972 to publish the works of His Divine Grace, has thus become the world's largest publisher of books in the field of Indian religion and philosophy. By the end of 1991, 450 million copies had been sold.

Before he passed away on the 14th of November 1977, Śrīla Prabhupāda had guided ISKCON and seen it grow to a world-wide confederation of more than one hundred *āśramas,* schools, temples, institutes, and farm communities.

The Artist

Madam Li Yuen Sheng was born in the city of Tientsin in Hopei, China, in 1924. Her interest in painting began in early childhood, and she studied under Mr. Chen Shao Mei, an accomplished artist, before graduating from Peking's Central Academy of Arts in 1950. Subsequently she worked as a graphic designer, but her reputation as an artist spread quickly, and in 1959 she was elected a member of the Chinese Painting Research Institute.

The paintings in this book bear the most recent witness to her excellence in the traditional Gongbi painting school style. They are the culmination of a remarkable career, during which her paintings were highly acclaimed by the celebrated Chinese artist Xu Bei Hong and exhibited by the Chinese Government both inside and outside of China. When she left China for Hong Kong in 1979, she was unable to take any of her paintings with her, because by that time they were considered part of the Chinese Art Treasury. Since then, the Hong Kong public has enjoyed exhibitions of her paintings at Shatin Municipal Hall and Star House at Tsim Sha Tsui. Her work has also been the topic of several newspaper and magazine articles.

The Gongbi style is very intricate in its finely detailed depiction of Chinese figures and scenery, as can be seen from the meticulous care and labour in Madam Li's work. It is only after a lifetime of practice and experience that she has acquired such a skillful hand. Now she is dedicating much of her time to teaching students who are interested in learning and preserving this fine painting tradition of which she is one of the few remaining masters.

Glossary

A

A. C. Bhaktivedanta Swami Prabhupāda — Founder-*ācārya* of the International Society for Krishna Consciousness and translator/ commentator of *Bhagavad-gītā, Śrīmad Bhāgavatam, Śrī Caitanya-caritāmṛta* and numerous other volumes of Vedic literatures.

Acintya-bhedābheda-tattva — the philosophy of simultaneous oneness and difference of the living entity in relation to the Absolute Truth, presented by Śrī Caitanya Mahāprabhu.

Akṣara — infallible living beings who are eternally situated in the spiritual abode.

Arcir-mārga — sun-line on the way to the spiritual planets.

Āśrama — one of the four spiritual orders of life: *brahmacārī-āśrama,* or student life; *gṛhastha-āśrama,* or married life; *vānaprastha-āśrama,* or retired life; and *sannyāsa-āśrama,* or the renounced order of life.

Asuras — (*a* — not + *sura* — godly) demon, or one who does not follow the principles of scripture.

B

Bhagavad-gītā — the essence of the Vedic scriptures, meaning 'song of God'. This literature was sung by Lord Kṛṣṇa to His disciple Arjuna in order to dissipate nescience.

Bhakti-yoga — the system of cultivation of *bhakti,* or pure devotional service, which is untinged by sense gratification or philosophical speculation.

Bhrūṇa-hatyā — killing the child in the womb as birth control.

Brahmā — the first created being in the universe.

Brahmacārī — celibate student under the care of a bona fide spiritual master.

Brāhmaṇas — the intelligent class of men, according to the system of four social and four spiritual orders.

C

Cāturmāsya — the four months of the summer rainy season.
Cikitsitam — well treated.

F

False ego — misidentification of the spirit soul with matter (the body and mind).

G

Gopīs — the cowherd girls of Vṛndāvana, pure devotees of Lord Śrī Kṛṣṇa.
Gorasa — milk, or the juice of the cow.
Guṇa — a material quality, of which there are three: ignorance, passion, and goodness; also string or rope.

K

Kaivalya — the absolute, as source of spirit and matter.
Kāmadhenus — cows of the spiritual abode.
Karma — fruitive action, for which there is always a reaction, good or bad.
Kṛpaṇa — one who is miserly and does not make use of valuable assets; specifically, one who wastes his life by not striving for spiritual realization.
Kṣatriyas — the administrators or protectors of society, according to the system of four social and four spiritual orders of life.
Kumud flowers — (*ku* — bad + *mud* — pleasure) flowers which do not take pleasure in sunrise.

M

Maṭhas — temples.
Māyā — (*mā* — not + *yā* — this) illusion; an energy of Kṛṣṇa which deludes the living entity into forgetfulness of the Supreme Lord.

Mukti — liberation, freedom from material consciousness, freedom from material desires.

P

Pitās — forefathers or ancestors.
Prasādam — foodstuffs offered to Śrī Kṛṣṇa.
Pratyāhāra — diversion, process by which *yoga* diverts our energies from external to internal.

R

Rajas — mode of passion of material nature.
Rasa — relationship between the Lord and the living entities.
Rāsa-līlā — pastime of Śrī Kṛṣṇa with the *gopīs* in Vṛndāvana.

S

Saṁsiddhi paramā — the highest perfection attained by the living entity who returns to Godhead and engages in personal service of the Lord.
Sanātana-dhāma — the eternal, spiritual abode.
Saṅkīrtana yajña — the sacrifice prescribed for the age of Kali, i.e. congregational chanting of the name, fame, and pastimes of the Supreme Personality of Godhead.
Śānta-rasa — the neutral relationship between the Lord and the living entities.
Sat — eternal.
Sattva — the mode of goodness of material nature.
Soma — a celestial beverage enjoyed by the residents of the moon.
Śrīmad-Bhāgavatam — the scripture composed by Vyāsadeva to describe and explain Lord Kṛṣṇa's pastimes.
Śūdras — labourers of society, according to the system of four social and four spiritual orders of life.

T

Tamas — the mode of ignorance of material nature.

U

Ugra-karma — (*ugra* — hard or difficult + *karma* — task) overly largescale and difficult type of industry and trade.

V

Vaiśyas — those involved in business and farming, according to the system of four social and four spiritual orders of life.

Varṇāśrama system — the system of four social orders and four spiritual orders of society.

Vedānta — (*veda* — knowledge + *ānta* — end) the end of all knowledge, or the scriptures containing knowledge of all branches of science, especially the science of spiritual self-realization.

Y

Yajña — sacrifice.

Yoga — the linking of the consciousness of the infinitesimal living entity with the supreme living entity, Kṛṣṇa.

Yuga — age or period in cosmic time.

The International Society for Krishna Consciousness
Founder-Acarya: His Divine Grace A.C. Bhaktivedanta Swami Prabhupada

CENTERS IN NORTH AMERICA

(September 1997)

CANADA

Calgary, Alberta — 313 Fourth Street N.E., T2E 3S3/ Tel. (403) 265-3302
Edmonton, Alberta — 9353 35th Avenue, T6E 5R5/ Tel. (403) 439-9999
Montreal, Quebec — 1626 Pie IX Boulevard, H1V 2C5/ Tel. (514) 521-1301
Ottawa, Ontario — 212 Somerset St. E., K1N 6V4/ Tel. (613) 565-6544
Regina, Saskatchewan — 1279 Retallack St., S4T 2H8/ Tel. (306) 525-1640
Toronto, Ontario — 243 Avenue Rd., M5R 2J6/ Tel. (416) 922-5415
Vancouver, B.C. — 5462 S.E. Marine Dr., Burnaby V5J 3G8/ Tel. (604) 433-9728
Victoria, B.C. — 1350 Lang St., V8T 2S5/ Tel. (604) 920-0026

FARM COMMUNITY

Ashcroft, B.C. — Saranagati Dhama, Box 99, V0K 1A0

ADDITIONAL RESTAURANT

Vancouver — Hare Krishna Place, 46 Begbie St., New Westminster

U.S.A.

Atlanta, Georgia — 1287 South Ponce de Leon Ave. N.E., 30306/ Tel. (404) 378-9234
Austin, Texas — 807-A E. 30th St., 78705/ Tel. (512) 320-0477/ E-mail: sankarsana@aol.com
Baltimore, Maryland — 200 Bloomsbury Ave., Catonsville, 21228/ Tel. (410) 744-1624 or 4069
Boise, Idaho — 1615 Martha St., 83706/ Tel. (208) 344-4274
Boston, Massachusetts — 72 Commonwealth Ave., 02116/ Tel. (617) 247-8611
Chicago, Illinois — 1716 W. Lunt Ave., 60626/ Tel. (312) 973-0900
Columbus, Ohio — 379 W. Eighth Ave., 43201/ Tel. (614) 421-1661
Dallas, Texas — 5430 Gurley Ave., 75223/ Tel. (214) 827-6330
Denver, Colorado — 1400 Cherry St., 80220/ Tel. (303) 333-5461
Detroit, Michigan — 383 Lenox Ave., 48215/ Tel. (313) 824-6000
Gainesville, Florida — 214 N.W. 14th St., 32603/ Tel. (904) 336-4183
Gurabo, Puerto Rico — HC01-Box 8440, 00778-9763/ Tel. (809) 737-1658
Hartford, Connecticut — 1683 Main St., E. Hartford, 06108/ Tel. (860) 289-7252
Honolulu, Hawaii — 51 Coelho Way, 96817/ Tel. (808) 595-3947
Houston, Texas — 1320 W. 34th St., 77018/ Tel. (713) 686-4482
Laguna Beach, California — 285 Legion St., 92651/ Tel. (714) 494-7029
Long Island, New York — 197 S. Ocean Avenue, Freeport, 11520/ Tel. (516) 223-4909
Los Angeles, California — 3764 Watseka Ave., 90034/ Tel. (310) 836-2676
Miami, Florida — 3220 Virginia St., 33133 (mail: P.O. Box 337, Coconut Grove, FL 33233)/Tel. (305) 442-7218
New Orleans, Louisiana — 2936 Esplanade Ave., 70119/ Tel. (504) 486-3583
New York, New York — 305 Schermerhorn St., Brooklyn, 11217/ Tel. (718) 855-6714
New York, New York — 26 Second Avenue, 10003/ Tel. (212) 420-1130
Philadelphia, Pennsylvania — 41 West Allens Lane, 19119/ Tel. (215) 247-4600
Phoenix, Arizona — 100 S. Weber Dr., Chandler, 85226/ Tel. (602) 705-4900/ Fax: (602) 705-4901
Portland, Oregon — 5137 N.E. 42 Ave., 97218/ Tel. (503) 287-3252
St. Louis, Missouri — 3926 Lindell Blvd., 63108/ Tel. (314) 535-8085
San Diego, California — 1030 Grand Ave., Pacific Beach, 92109/ Tel. (619) 483-2500
Seattle, Washington — 1420 228th Ave. S.E., Issaquah, 98027/ Tel. (206) 391-3293
Tallahassee, Florida — 1323 Nylic St. (mail: P.O. Box 20224, 32304)/ Tel. (904) 681-9258
Towaco, New Jersey — P.O. Box 109, 07082/ Tel. (201) 299-0970
Tucson, Arizona — 711 E. Blacklidge Dr., 85719/ Tel. (520) 792-0630
Washington, D.C. — 3200 Ivy Way, Harwood, MD 20776/ Tel. (301) 261-4493
Washington, D.C. — 10310 Oaklyn Dr., Potomac, Maryland 20854/ Tel. (301) 299-2100

FARM COMMUNITIES

Alachua, Florida (New Raman Reti) — P.O. Box 819, 32615/ Tel. (904) 462-2017
Carriere, Mississippi (New Talavan) — 31492 Anner Road, 39426/ Tel. (601) 799-1354
Gurabo, Puerto Rico (New Govardhana Hill) — (contact ISKCON Gurabo)
Hillsborough, North Carolina (New Goloka) — 1032 Dimmocks Mill Rd., 27278/ Tel. (919) 732-6492
Moundsville, West Virginia (New Vrindaban) — R.D. No. 1, Box 319, Hare Krishna Ridge, 26042/ Tel. (304) 843-1600/ Fax: (304) 845-9819/ E-mail: story 108@juno.com; (lodging:) kisore@aol.com
Mulberry, Tennessee (Murari-sevaka) — Rt. No. 1, Box 146-A, 37359/ Tel (615) 759-6888
Port Royal, Pennsylvania (Gita Nagari) — R.D. No. 1, Box 839, 17082/ Tel. (717) 527-4101

ADDITIONAL RESTAURANTS AND DINING

Boise, Idaho — Govinda's, 500 W. Main St., 83702/ Tel. (208) 338-9710
Eugene, Oregon — Govinda's Vegetarian Buffet, 270 W. 8th St., 97401/ Tel. (503) 686-3531
Fresno, California — Govinda's, 2373 E. Shaw, 93710/ Tel. (209) 225-1230
Gainesville, Florida — Radha's, 125 NW 23rd Ave., 32609/ Tel. (904) 376-9012

BHAGAVAD-GITA AS IT IS

The World's Most Popular Edition of a Timeless Classic

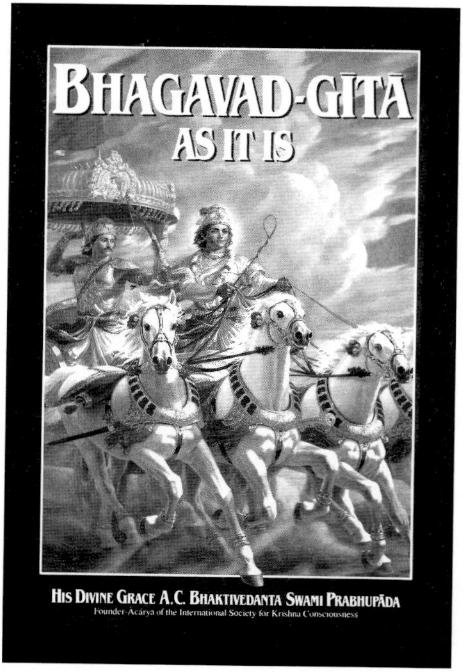

Throughout the ages, the world's greatest minds have turned to the *Bhagavad-gita* for answers to life's perennial questions. Renowned as the jewel of India's spiritual wisdom, the *Gita* summarizes the profound Vedic knowledge concerning man's essential nature, his environment, and ultimately his relationship with God. With more than fifty million copies sold in twenty languages, *Bhagavad-gita As It Is,* by His Divine Grace A. C. Bhaktivedanta Swami Prabhupada, is the most widely read edition of the *Gita* in the world. It includes the original Sanskrit text, phonetic transliterations, word-for-word meanings, translation, elaborate commentary, and many full-colour illustrations.

	Soft	Vinyl	Hard	Deluxe
UK	**£4.00**	**£6.50**	**£7.95**	**£13.95**
US	$3.90	$8.50	$10.30	$18.00
AUS		$11.00	$14.00	$28.00

EASY JOURNEY TO OTHER PLANETS

One of Srila Prabhupada's earliest books *Easy Journey* describes how *bhakti-yoga* enables us to transfer ourselves from the material to the spiritual world.

Softbound, 96 pages

UK: £1.50; US: $1.00; AUS: $2.00

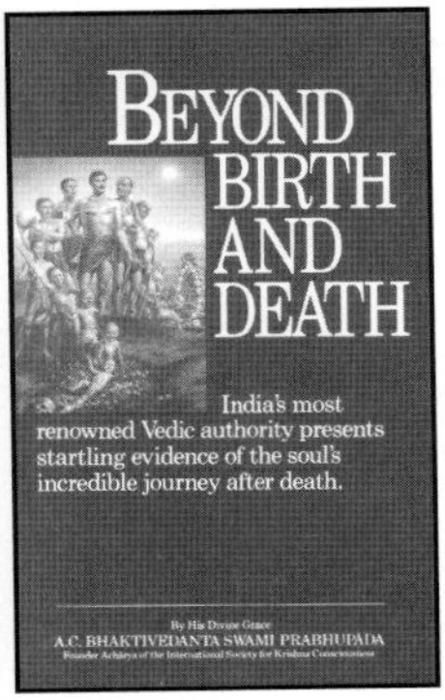

BEYOND BIRTH AND DEATH

What is the self? Can it exist apart from the physical body? If so, what happens to the self at the time of death? What about reincarnation? Liberation? *Beyond Birth and Death* answers these intriguing questions and more.

Softbound, 96 pages

UK: £1.50, US: $1.00; AUS: $2.00

THE HIGHER TASTE

A Guide to Gourmet Vegetarian Cooking and a Karma-Free Diet

Illustrated profusely with black-and-white drawings and eight full-colour plates, this popular volume contains over 60 tried and tested international recipes, together with the why's and how's of the Krishna conscious vegetarian life-style.

Softbound, 176 pages

UK: £1.50; US: $1.99; AUS: $2.00

RAJA-VIDYA: THE KING OF KNOWLEDGE

In this book we learn why knowledge of Krishna is absolute and frees the soul from material bondage.

Softbound, 128 pages

UK: £1.50; US: $1.00; AUS: $2.00

THE PERFECTION OF YOGA

A lucid explanation of the psychology, techniques, and purposes of *yoga*, a summary and comparison of the different *yoga* systems, and an introduction to meditation.

Softbound, 96 pages

UK: £1.50; US: $1.00; AUS: $2.00

COMING BACK

Coming Back answers the most profound and mysterious of all questions by presenting clear and complete explanations from the world's most authentic, timeless sources of knowledge about the afterlife. With this book you will learn the science of controlling your present, determining your future, and dramatically changing your life!

Softbound, 160 pages, 16 colour pages

UK: £1.50; US: $1.00; AUS: $2.00

GREAT VEGETARIAN DISHES

Featuring over 100 stunning full-colour photos, this new book is for spiritually aware people who want the exquisite taste of Hare Krishna cooking without a lot of time in the kitchen. The 240 international recipes were tested and refined by world-famous Hare Krishna chef Kurma dasa.

240 recipes, 192 pages, coffee table size hardback

UK: £12.95; US: $19.95; AUS: $24.95

THE HARE KRISHNA BOOK OF VEGETARIAN COOKING

A colourfully illustrated, practical cookbook that not only helps you prepare authentic Indian dishes at home, but also teaches you about the ancient tradition behind India's world-famous vegetarian cuisine.

130 kitchen-tested recipes, 300 pages, hardback

UK: £12.95; US: $11.60; AUS: $15.00

Order Form

Make check or money order payable to The Bhaktivedanta Book Trust and send to:

The Bhaktivedanta Book Trust
Dept. DHA-H
3764 Watseka Avenue • Los Angeles, CA 90034

Name ____
Please Print

Address ____

City ______________________ ST ______ Zip ______________

Code	Description	Qty.	Price	Total

Subtotal US $ ______________

CA Sales Tax 8.25% US $ ______________

Shipping 15% of Subtotal (minimum $2.00) US $ ______________

TOTAL US $ ______________

To Place a Credit Card Order Please Call

1-800-927-4152

VISA MasterCard

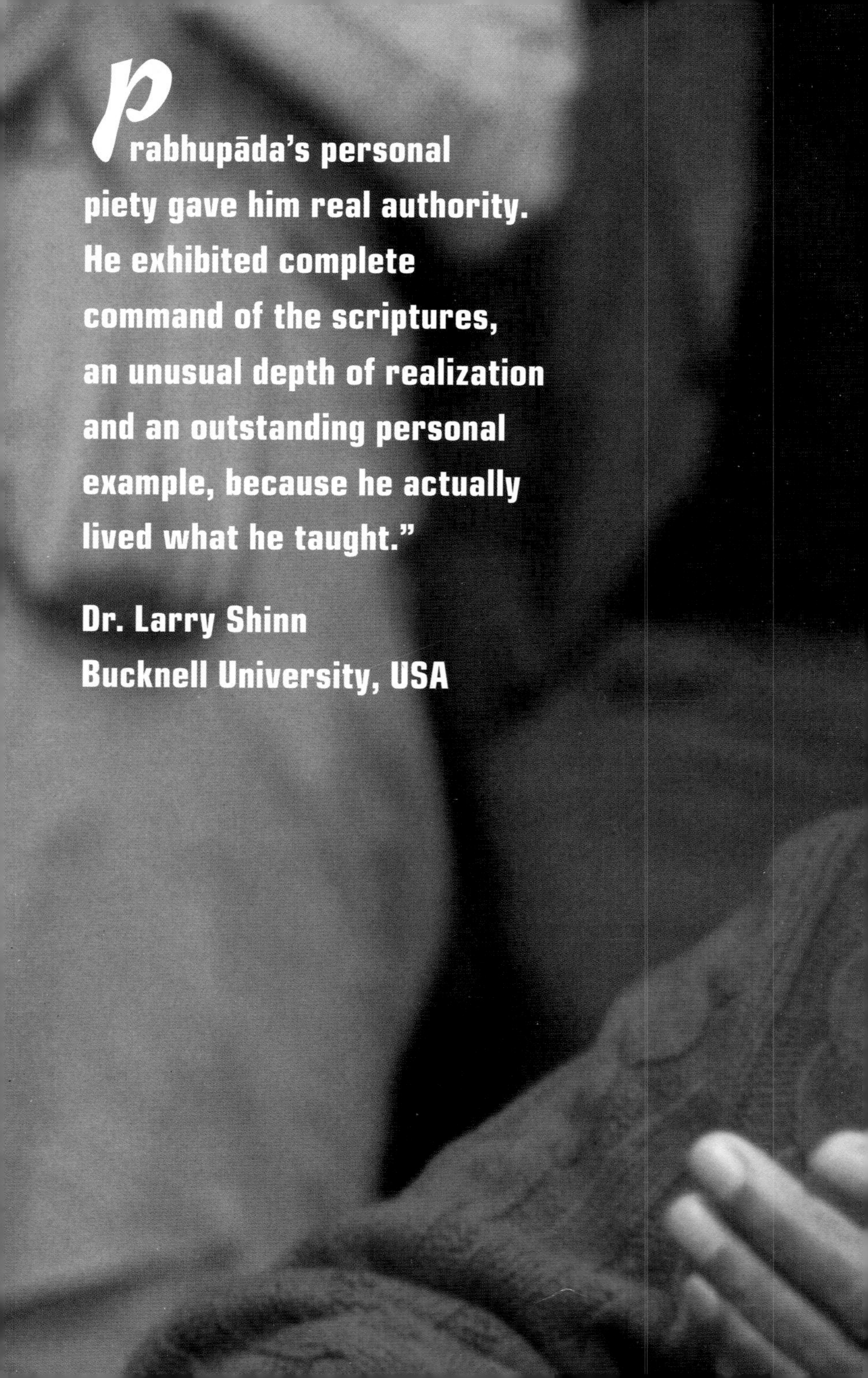

Prabhupāda's personal piety gave him real authority. He exhibited complete command of the scriptures, an unusual depth of realization and an outstanding personal example, because he actually lived what he taught."

Dr. Larry Shinn
Bucknell University, USA